THE WORLD IN ANCIENT TIMES

PRIMARY SOURCES AND REFERENCE VOLUME

RONALD MELLOR &
AMANDA H. PODANY
GENERAL EDITORS

THE WORLD IN ANCIENT TIMES

PRIMARY SOURCES AND REFERENCE VOLUME

Ronald Mellor & Amanda H. Podany

For my dear friends Eric and Judy Monkkonen—R.M.
For my parents, Margaret and Brian Hills—A.P.

OXFORD
UNIVERSITY PRESS

Oxford University Press, Inc., publishes works that further
Oxford University's objective of excellence
in research, scholarship, and education.

Oxford New York
Auckland Cape Town Dar es Salaam Hong Kong Karachi
Kuala Lumpur Madrid Melbourne Mexico City Nairobi
New Delhi Shanghai Taipei Toronto

With offices in
Argentina Austria Brazil Chile Czech Republic France Greece
Guatemala Hungary Italy Japan Poland Portugal Singapore
South Korea Switzerland Thailand Turkey Ukraine Vietnam

Published by Oxford University Press, Inc.
198 Madison Avenue, New York, New York 10016
www.oup.com

Series design: Stephanie Blumenthal
Volume design and layout: Alexis Siroc
Cover design and logo: Nora Wertz

Library of Congress Cataloging-in-Publication Data
Primary sources and reference volume / [edited by] Ronald Mellor &
Amanda H. Podany.
p. cm. — (The world in ancient times)
Includes index.
ISBN-10: 0-19-522220-2 (general edition isbn-10)
ISBN-13: 978-0-19-522220-3 (general edition isbn-13)
ISBN-10: 0-19-522301-2 (calif. edition isbn-10)
ISBN-13: 978-0-19-522301-9 (calif. edition isbn-13)

1. History, Ancient--Sources. 2. History, Ancient. 3.
Civilization, Ancient. I. Mellor, Ronald. II. Podany, Amanda H. III. Series.
D52.P75 2005
930--dc22
2004026578

Set ISBN-13: 978-0-19-522220-3 — ISBN-10: 0-19-522220-2

Printing number: 9 8 7 6 5 4 3 2 1

Printed in the United States of America
on acid-free paper

On the cover: This Mesopotamian sculpture of a dog from the beginning of the second millennium BCE was used to hold candles. The dog is covered with cuneiform writing.
Frontispiece: A cat with a shepherd's staff guards six geese and a nest of eggs in this scene from a fable painted about 1120 BCE in Egypt.

RONALD MELLOR &
AMANDA H. PODANY
GENERAL EDITORS

DIANE L. BROOKS, ED. D.
EDUCATION CONSULTANT

The Early Human World
Peter Robertshaw & Jill Rubalcaba

The Ancient Near Eastern World
Amanda H. Podany & Marni McGee

The Ancient Egyptian World
Eric H. Cline & Jill Rubalcaba

The Ancient South Asian World
Jonathan Mark Kenoyer & Kimberley Heuston

The Ancient Chinese World
Terry Kleeman & Tracy Barrett

The Ancient Greek World
Jennifer T. Roberts & Tracy Barrett

The Ancient Roman World
Ronald Mellor & Marni McGee

The Ancient American World
William Fash & Mary E. Lyons

The World in Ancient Times: Primary Sources and Reference Volume
Ronald Mellor & Amanda H. Podany

CONTENTS

A [“] marks a primary source—an ancient text or account of a discovery that speaks to us from the past.

SOME PRONUNCIATIONS

Abu Hureyra (A-boo hoo-RAIR-a)
Abydos (a-BEE-dos)
Akkad (AHK-ahd)
Alashiya (ahl-ah-SHEE-uh)
Amarna (uh-MAR-nuh)
Assyria (uh-SEER-ee-uh)
Babylon (BA-buh-lun)
Benares(buh-NAHR-us)
Bithynia (buh-THIN-ee-uh)
Carthage (KAR-thij)
Çatalhöyük (CHAH-tahl-HOO-yook)
Chu (choo)
Crete (kreet)
Corduba (KORD-yuh-buh)
Cuzco (KOO-sko)
Deir el-Medina (DARE el-muh-DEE-nuh)
Dilmun (DIL-mun)
Galatia (guh-LAY-shee-uh)
Hatti (HAH-tee)
Karnak (KAR-nak)
Mittani (mih-TAH-nee)
Olduvai Gorge (OHL-duh-way)
Pataliputra (PAHT-uh-lih-POO-truh)
Pompeii (pahm-PAY)
Punjab (puhn-JAHB)
Qadesh (ka-DESH)
Qi (chee)
Tenochtitlan (tay-NOTCH-tee-TLAN)
Uruk (UR-uhk)
Wei (way)
Wu (woo)
Xi'an (shee-ahn)
Yangzi River (yahng-dzuh)

THE WORLD IN ANCIENT TIMES

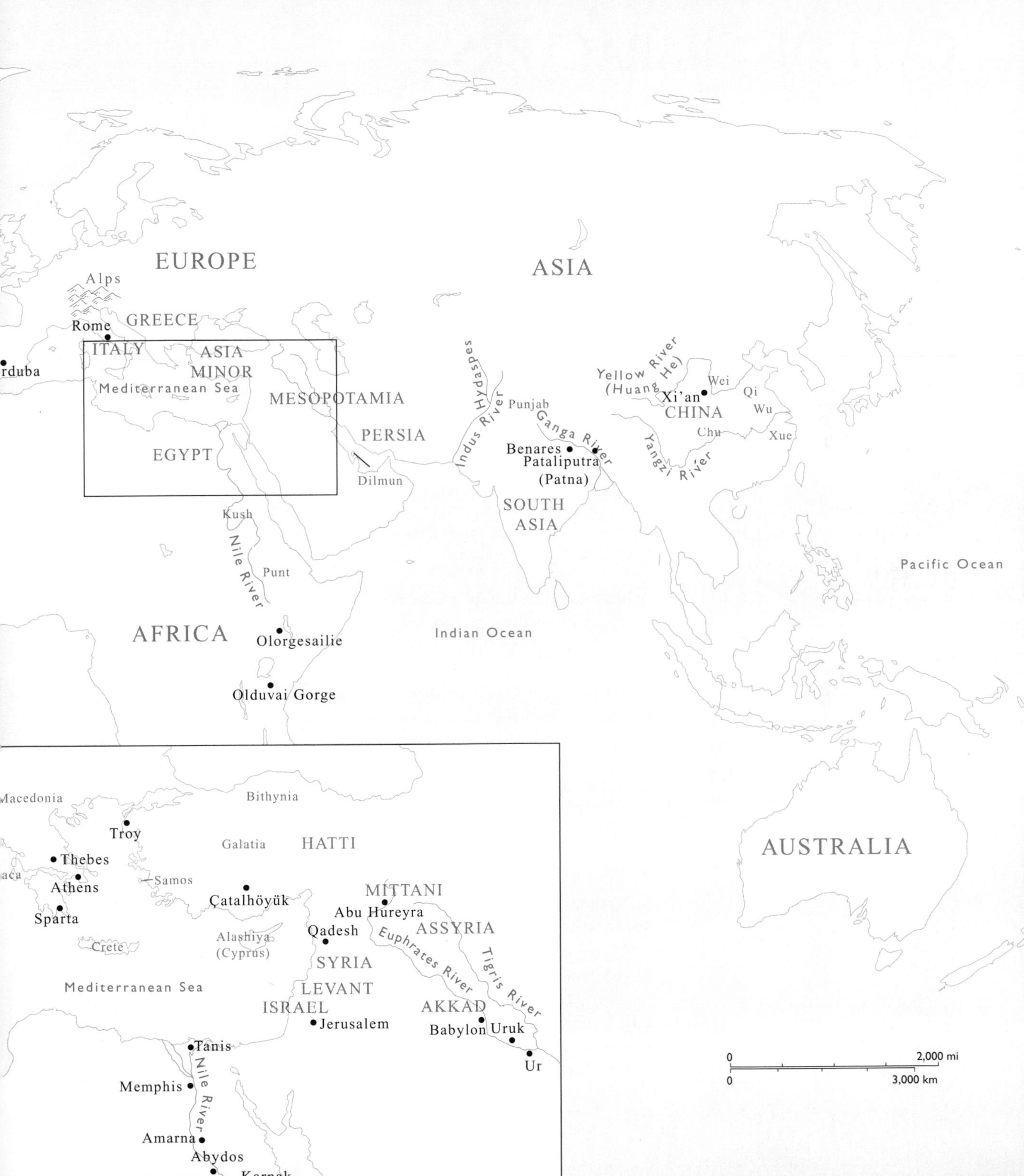

EUROPE
ASIA
Alps
GREECE
Rome
ITALY
ASIA
MINOR
rduba
Mediterranean Sea
MESOPOTAMIA
PERSIA
EGYPT
Dilmun
Kush
Nile River
Punt
Hydaspes
Indus River
Punjab
Ganga River
Benares
Pataliputra
(Patna)
SOUTH
ASIA
Yellow River
(Huang He)
Xi'an
Wei
Qi
Wu
CHINA
Chu
Xue
Yangzi River
Pacific Ocean
AFRICA
Olorgesailie
Indian Ocean
Olduvai Gorge
AUSTRALIA
Macedonia
Bithynia
Troy
Galatia
HATTI
Thebes
Athens
Samos
Sparta
Çatalhöyük
MITTANI
Abu Hureyra
ASSYRIA
Qadesh
Crete
Alashiya
(Cyprus)
SYRIA
Euphrates River
Tigris River
Mediterranean Sea
LEVANT
ISRAEL
AKKAD
Jerusalem
Babylon
Uruk
Ur
Tanis
Nile River
Memphis
Amarna
Abydos
Karnak
Valley of the Kings
Deir el-Medina
Thebes
0
2,000 mi
0
3,000 km

CAST OF CHARACTERS

Because The World in Ancient Times *covers many cultures, we use the abbreviations* CE *for "Common Era" and* BCE *for "Before the Common Era." The traditional equivalents are* BC *for "Before Christ" and* AD *for* "Anno Domini," *Latin for "In the Year of Our Lord," referring to the birth of Jesus Christ.*

Aeneas (ay-NEE-us) • Legendary Trojan prince, son of goddess Venus, who sailed to Italy to establish the Roman people

Aesop (EE-sop), sixth century BCE • Greek slave and storyteller

Akhenaten (ahk-ken-NAH-ton), 1350–1334 BCE • Heretic king of Egypt; replaced the gods of Egypt with the worship of a single god, Aten (the sun disk).

Alexander the Great, 356–323 BCE • Greek ruler, from 336 to 323 BCE, who conquered Egypt, Persia, and northern India; son of Philip of Macedon

Amenhotep III (ah-men-HOE-tep), also called **Nimmureya** (nim-oo-RAY-uh), ruled 1387–1350 BCE • Egyptian king who married Princess Tadu-Heba of Syria

Antigone (an-TIG-uh-nee) • Daughter of Oedipus in Greek mythology

Aphrodite (AF-ruh-DIE-tee) • Goddess of love in Greek mythology

Aristotle (AR-i-stah-tl), 384–322 BCE • Greek philosopher and teacher; founded the Lyceum

Arjuna (AHR-jun) • South Asian warrior prince who is the hero of the Bhagavad Gita

Arrian (AIR-ee-un), second century CE• Greek historian

Aten (AH-ten) • Egyptian god representing the sun's disk

Athena (uh-THEE-nuh) • Goddess of war and wisdom in Greek mythology, patron deity of Athens

Beder (BAY-dare), 11th century BCE • Prince of the town of Dor in the Levant

Brahma (BRAH-mu) • The greatest of the South Asian Vedic gods, he is All

Buddha (BOOD-ah), about 563–483 BCE • Born Prince **Siddhartha Gautama** (si-DARTH-a GOW-tam-a) in what is now Nepal; founded Buddhism

Cao Cao (tsow tsow), 155–220 CE • General and poet who effectively ruled China during the last 15 years of the Han dynasty

Chandra Gupta II (CHUN-drah GOOP-ta), reigned 376–415 BCE • Greatest ruler of the Gupta era, a time when the arts flourished in India

Chandragupta Maurya (CHUN-drah-goop-ta MAOW-rya), reigned 321–297 BCE • One of India's great leaders, founder of the Mauryan dynasty

Charles I, King of Spain, 1516–1556, also Charles V, Holy Roman emperor • Presided over the conquest of Mexico and Peru

Confucius (con-FYU-shus) or **Kong Qiu** (koong chyoh), 551–479 BCE • China's first philosopher

Cortés (cor-TESS), **Hernán** (err-NAHN), 1485–1547 CE • Explorer who conquered Aztec empire for Spain

Cuauhtemoc (kwow-TEH-moke), 1496–1524 CE • Aztec emperor who succeeded his uncle Moctezuma; the Spanish captured him in 1521 and executed him in 1524

Daedalus (DED-l-us) • Architect in Greek mythology who made wings out of birds' feathers and wax

David, around 1000 BCE • King of Israel who united the Israelite people; made Jerusalem his capital city

de León (deh lay-OAN), **Pedro de Cieza** (PEH-dro deh see-AY-sah), 1522–54 CE • Spanish chronicler of the Inca world

Enheduanna (en-HEH-doo-AH-nah), 24th century BCE • High priestess of the moon god in Mesopotamia; first-known author in history

Faxian (fah-SHYEN) • Buddhist monk from China who traveled to India (from 399 to 414 CE) to visit sacred shrines and collect manuscripts

Gilgamesh (GIL-guh-mesh), around 2600 BCE • Mesopotamian king of Uruk, whose legendary adventures are recorded in the *Epic of Gilgamesh*

Hammurabi (hahm-oo-RAH-bee), ruled 1792–1750 BCE • King of Babylon who built an empire; best known for his collection of laws

Hatshepsut (hat-SHEP-soot), also known as **Makere** (ma-KAY-ray), ruled 1498–1483 BCE • Female king of Egypt; ruled in place of her stepson Thutmose III for nearly 20 years

Hector • Trojan hero in the Greek epic the *Iliad*

Herodotus (huh-RAH-duh-tus), about 484–420 BCE • Greek historian who wrote *Histories,* about the Persian wars

Homer, eighth century BCE • Greek epic poet who wrote the *Iliad* and the *Odyssey*

Horace (HOR-iss), 65–8 BCE • Latin lyric poet

Inanna (ih-NAH-nah) • Mesopotamian goddess of love and war

Jesus of Nazareth, 4 BCE–29 CE • Proclaimed Messiah (Christ) by his followers in Palestine

Jia Kui (jyah kway), 30–101 CE • Chinese scholar who could recite the classics by memory at age 19; only a few quotations from his writing survive today

Kalidasa (KAH-lee-DAH-sah), fifth century CE • India's greatest playwright, author of *Sakuntala*

Kautilya (kaow-TIL-yuh), fourth and third centuries BCE • Chandragupta Maurya's great political adviser, author of the *Arthashastra*

Krishna (KRISH-nah) • One of the forms of the South Asian god Vishnu

Leakey, Louis, 1903–72 • African-born anthropologist who excavated in East Africa, particularly Olduvai Gorge

Leakey, Mary, 1913–96 • English archaeologist who uncovered the early hominid footprints at Laetoli and excavated Olduvai Gorge in Tanzania

King Li (lee) **of Zhou** (joe), ruled 857–842 BCE • Cruel Western Zhou king in ancient China whose people criticized him

Liu Xiang (lyoe shyahng), 77–6 BCE • Member of the Han royal family and imperial librarian, he compiled China's first bibliography and edited many manuscripts from earlier times

Liu Yiqing (lyoe yee-ching) 403–444 CE • Chinese prince who compiled the *New Account of Tales of the World*

Manco Capac (MAHN-ko KAH-pahk) • Legendary first king of the Incas

Manu (MAH-noo) • Founder of the human race in South Asian mythology who was believed to have dictated early laws

Lord Mengchang (muhng-chahng) • Patron of scholars and aristocrat of the state of Qi in the Warring States period (476–206 BCE)

Moctezuma II (MOKE-teh-zoo-mah), about 1467–1520 CE • Aztec emperor captured by Spaniards

Nanna (NAH-nah) also known as **Sin** • Mesopotamian god of the moon whose main city was Ur

Nebmare-nakht (NEB-mar-ray NAHKT), about 12th or 11th century BCE • Scribe who lived during Egypt's Dynasty 20 and wrote a description of the life of a scribe, now called Papyrus Lansing

Nero (NEER-oh), 37–68 CE • Roman emperor from 54 to 68 CE

Odysseus (oh-DIS-ee-us) • Mythical Greek hero of Homer's *Odyssey*

Ötzi (OOT-see) **the Iceman,** 5,300 years ago • A well-preserved corpse of a man shot in the back with a bow and arrow, found in the Alps

Ovid (AW-vid), 43 BCE–17 CE • Roman poet who wrote of love and mythology in a long poem called *Metamorphoses*

Pausanias (paw-SAY-nee-us), second century CE • Greek travel writer; he wrote *Description of Greece*

Pericles (PAIR-ih-kleez), about 495–429 BCE • Athenian statesman who reformed laws to give lower classes more power, for a more democratic society

Pheidias (FID-ee-us), fifth century BCE • Greek sculptor

Piye (PEE-yee), 747–716 BCE • King of Kush and then of Egypt; thought to be the first king of Egypt's Dynasty 25

Plato (PLAY-toh), about 427–347 BCE • Greek philosopher and teacher who founded the Academy, a school in Athens, and wrote the *Republic*

Pliny the Younger (PLIN-ee), about 62–113 CE • Roman orator and statesman, nephew of Pliny the Elder

Plutarch (PLOO-tark), 46–after 119 CE • Roman biographer and essayist

Porus (POHR-us), fourth century BCE • Indian king and opponent of Alexander the Great

Ptah-hotep (tah-HOE-tep), 23rd century BCE • Egyptian vizier during the Old Kingdom

Quetzalcoatl (ket-zahl-CO-ahtl) • Important Mesoamerican god; his name means "Feathered Serpent"

Qin Shi Huangdi (chin shur hwahng-dee), also known as Ying Zheng (ing juhng), ruled 246–210 BCE • First emperor of Qin in China

Ramesses II (RAM-ah-seas), 1279–1212 BCE • King of Egypt; fought against the Hittites; ruled for nearly 70 years and had many wives, concubines, and children

Saul, 11th century BCE • First king of Israel, who often fought against the Philistines, according to the Hebrew Bible

Sennacherib (sen-NAH-keh-rib), ruled 704–681 BCE • Assyrian king who destroyed Babylon

Shao, Duke of, about 840 BCE • Chinese duke and adviser to King Li, who saved the life of the king's son, the future King Xuan, by offering his own son in his place

Siddhartha (see Buddha)

Sima Qian (suh-ma chee-yen) ruled 221–210 BCE • Chinese historian and author of *Records of the Historian,* a history of everything that happened in China up to his time

Sinuhe (SIN-oo-way), about 1991–1926 BCE • Egyptian traveler, possibly fictional; story of his wanderings and life takes place during the reigns of Kings Amenemhet and Senwosert

Socrates (SOCK-ruh-teez), about 470–399 BCE • Greek philosopher who invented a question-and-answer form of teaching called the Socratic method

Tacitus (TAS-ih-tus), about 55–117 CE • Roman historian and biographer

Telemachus (tel-EM-ak-us) • Son of Odysseus and prince of Ithaca in Greek mythology

Temilotzin (teh-me-LOT-zin), about 1495–1525 CE • Aztec poet and friend of the Aztec prince, Cuauhtemoc, with whom he was captured; Temilotzin's poetry survives in the Nahuatl language

Thucydides (thoo-SID-ih-deez), about 460–after 404 BCE • Greek historian who wrote *History of the Peloponnesian War*

Trajan (TRAY-jun), 53–117 CE • Roman emperor from 98 to 117 CE

Tushratta (toosh-RAH-tah), 14th century BCE • King of Mittani, an ancient Syrian kingdom

Virgil (VUR-juhl), 70–19 BCE • Roman poet who wrote the epic *Aeneid*

Vishnu (VISH-noo) • One of the three major Brahmanical gods in India; considered "the Preserver," he often appears in different forms

Wang Jia (wahng jyah) • Chinese author of *Record of Forgotten Things*; described as rude and ugly but quick witted and fond of making pronouncements

Wenamun (WEN-ah-mun), about 1098–1070 BCE • Egyptian traveler, possibly fictional; story of his journey to the cities of Dor and Byblos, in what are now modern Israel and Lebanon, takes place at the end of the New Kingdom period

Xuan (shwen) of **Chu** (choo), ruled 369–340 BCE • Chinese king of Chu in mid-fourth century

Zeus (zoose) • Mythical son of Cronos and chief god of the Greeks

INTRODUCTION: DETECTIVES EXPLORING THE ANCIENT WORLD

During January of 1902, right at the start of a new century, French archaeologists were excavating at the ancient city of Susa in Iran. This city was inhabited for a long, long time—more than 5,000 years. If you could have visited it 3,500 years ago, you would have seen towering temples and palaces, magnificent city gates and fine houses, and people everywhere going about their daily business. But for more than 700 years, Susa had been abandoned, and by 1902 all that was left was a vast mound of dirt in the middle of a desolate plain.

Jacques DeMorgan, the director of the excavations that year, was anxious to find wonderful objects to take back to Paris. He instructed hundreds of workmen to dig enormous trenches through the site. They found what he wanted—hundreds of objects that ancient people had made—but they mostly ignored the remains of the ancient buildings where they were dug up. This would never happen on an excavation today. Archaeologists now know how important it is to record exactly where an object is found and what is around it in order to really understand it.

Among the artifacts uncovered that winter was one that took DeMorgan's breath away: a seven-foot-high monument, almost perfectly preserved, made out of polished black stone. You can imagine his excitement as this huge object was hauled out of the trench after thousands of years. At the top was an image, carved in relief (an art form where a picture is cut into a flat surface), of a man standing, his hand raised in prayer, in front of a seated god. Under this image were hundreds of lines of beautifully carved cuneiform writing, the wedge-shaped script used thousands of years ago in Mesopotamia.

Scholars immediately recognized the importance of the monument, and within months the cuneiform text had been translated and published: here were the Laws of Hammurabi, king of Babylon in the 18th century BCE, carved during the reign of the king himself. They were some of the earliest written laws in the world.

Hammurabi's collection of laws is a primary source for the study of ancient Mesopotamia. That means that it was produced during ancient times and gives us direct evidence for the history of the time. As with any ancient text or artifact (including buildings and tools, for example), both the relief sculpture at the top and the laws themselves are primary sources. In order to learn about the past, historians spend much of their time doing detective work: reading, examining, and analyzing primary sources.

On top of the stele on which his laws are carved, Hammurabi receives a rod from a seated god, showing that his right to rule has been granted by the gods.

A secondary source (so called becomes it comes second, written after the primary sources and based on them) is a book or article written by a historian who has studied a lot of primary sources. The writer tries to pull together all the pieces of evidence into an interesting and accurate account about the past. A textbook, for example, is a secondary source.

Historians, who write secondary sources, use almost anything they find from ancient times as a primary source. Most of the primary sources in this book were written down in ancient times and have been studied by historians. Some were originally written on stone, like Hammurabi's laws, some on clay, papyrus, or silk, some even on walls or animal bones. The ancient words have all been translated into English so that you can make sense of them, without knowing how to read cuneiform or hieroglyphs or ancient Chinese characters. Just think—the primary sources are the words of ancient people speaking directly to you. They can open up whole new worlds to you. But you have to read them carefully in order to understand those new worlds.

REPORTING LIVE FROM THE ANCIENT WORLD

When reading any primary source, you need to ask a number of questions to help you understand what the ancient writer can tell you. An old rule of thumb for reporters is to ask the five Ws: who, what, where, when, and why? The same questions apply when reading ancient texts. The first four questions will help you get your bearings. Ask yourself, "Who wrote this source? What type of document is it? When and where was it written?"

If the answers aren't clear from the source itself, you can find them in the introduction before each primary source. If you were to look at Hammurabi's laws in this book, you would learn from the introduction that King Hammurabi of Babylon was the author, that the document is a set of laws, which he wrote in the Akkadian language around 1755 BCE, and that they came from the ancient Mesopotamian civilization. Good. You can apply what you learn from reading the source to your understanding of that civilization.

You also need to ask yourself another "when" question. Was the source written at the same time as the events and ideas it describes? The source introduction tells us that no time passed between the reign of Hammurabi and the writing of this particular document. It's a true depiction of his times. If the date of the document had been, say, 200 years after Hammurabi's death, you would need to be a little more skeptical. People don't remember things very well after 200 years—they are writing down ideas that they've heard from their parents, who heard them from their parents, who heard them from their parents. . . . You can imagine how many mistakes slip in. Now you need to ask yourself another "who" question. Who was the author writing for? Did the author have an audience in mind or was he writing just for himself?

Well, if this had been a diary, Hammurabi probably would have been writing for himself. (Unfortunately, as far as we know, he never wrote one.) If it had been a letter, then he would have been writing for the person he was sending it to (quite a few of his letters do survive). In both cases, you could expect the source to be pretty accurate. Hammurabi wouldn't have expected those types of documents to last or to be read by a big audience, so he probably wouldn't have exaggerated his accounts. But *this* one is different.

Hammurabi wrote in the last section of the laws, the epilogue, "I have inscribed my precious pronouncements upon my stela [monument] and set it up before the statue of me, the king of justice, in the city of Babylon." Obviously, he was writing for an audience, and it was a big one: the whole city of Babylon. So he would have wanted to make sure that he came off well. He wouldn't have written anything along the lines of "Hammurabi, who really isn't sure what to do with his empire right now, who has a painful knee, and would really like a break from being king for a while." No, you never see a king write anything like that in public. He wrote instead that he was "the king of justice" and "the able king." *Was* he an able king? He thought so, but we can't judge from this document alone.

Now you have to ask yourself perhaps the most important of the five questions: why was this document written? Hammurabi tells us in the epilogue exactly why he wrote the laws: "In order that the mighty not wrong the weak, to provide just ways for the orphan and the widow." He wanted to be fair to people who weren't powerful in society. What a nice guy. But there's something else going on here. He writes that a man who wants to bring a lawsuit should have someone read the laws to him (which means that most people couldn't read). He also writes, "may he examine his case, may he calm his troubled heart, and may he praise me." Hmm. So the bottom line is that Hammurabi wanted to be praised for this. That was probably a big part of the reason why the laws were written and set up in public: not only would the people have a fair system of justice, but people would also "praise" and approve of the job that Hammurabi was doing as king.

Even the sculpture at the top of the monument tells us a story. It shows Hammurabi praying in front of a seated god. The picture is telling his people (even the ones who couldn't read) that he was a religious man. And the god is handing him something: a rod and a ring. Mesopotamians would have recognized these as symbols of leadership. So Hammurabi's right to rule, according to him, came from the gods.

DETECTIVE HISTORIAN ON THE CASE

Now your work as a reporter is finished. You've found the answers to who, what, when, where, and why. But your job isn't done; it's time to become a detective, the most important part of a historian's work. The documents we have from the ancient world are like clues in a mystery. The historian has to figure out what the clues mean and what they tell us about the ancient culture. Just as a detective tries to find more than one witness to a crime, to get more than one version of the events, a historian asks, "Are there other primary sources written about this same subject?"

Hammurabi thought he was pretty terrific, but was it true? Fortunately, we don't just have his word for it. Lots of documents were written about Hammurabi, during his lifetime and after his death. Although he certainly had some enemies, most of the documents show that Hammurabi was indeed considered to be a fair and able king.

Now we have to ask ourselves what this document, or clue, tells us about this ancient culture. Well, we know already from the epilogue that the Mesopotamian people cared about justice, that Hammurabi had a lot of power, and that most people couldn't read. And we know from the relief sculpture that the king was religious and claimed that the gods had given him the right to rule.

What can the laws tell us? Law number 22 states: “If a man commits a robbery and is then seized, that man shall be killed.” That seems pretty straightforward. This was a land that had the death penalty, and it was applied in cases of robbery. We don’t, however, know *how* the death penalty was carried out (and the laws never mention what was the usual way).

The very next law, number 23, says: “If the robber should not be seized, the man who has been robbed shall establish the extent of his lost property before the god; and the city and the governor in whose territory and district the robbery was committed shall replace his lost property to him.” Got it? Perhaps not—it’s a little confusing. You need to think this one through carefully. What’s going on here?

Imagine that the man who was robbed lost a bag of silver, maybe his whole life savings. The robber hadn’t been caught, so there was nothing that the law could do to him, but you still had a victim who had lost a lot of property. Would he have to suffer being poor now just because he was robbed? No. The law states that the government of the place where he was robbed must give him the same amount of silver that was taken from him. This seems generous. Perhaps the king viewed the robbery as partly the fault of the local government, because they didn’t keep the streets safe enough.

How did they know how much silver he lost, though? Perhaps no one else saw how much silver was in the bag that day. So the victim had to establish it “before the god.” That means he had to stand in front of the statue of a god and swear to how much silver he lost. Why didn’t he just lie and say that he lost pounds and pounds more silver than he really did? There must have been a good reason for the king to trust that he wouldn’t do this. We can guess (and be right) that people feared that the god would punish them if they lied under oath.

So now we know a lot more about Mesopotamia in Hammurabi’s time. We know that the king cared about the rights of victims, that people believed that the gods could judge if someone was lying or not, and that a local government was responsible for compensating victims for crimes that took place in their region. All from two laws!

Hammurabi's laws covered many different situations, even ones that don't sound much like crimes to us. Here's law 148, in two different translations:

1955 translation	1997 translation
When a seignior married a woman and a fever has then seized her, if he has made up his mind to marry another, he may marry her, without divorcing his wife whom the fever seized; she shall live in the house which he built and he shall continue to support her as long as she lives.	If a man marries a woman and later a skin disease seizes her and he decides to marry another woman, he will not divorce his wife whom the skin disease seized; she shall reside in quarters he constructs and he shall continue to support her as long as she lives.

The basic idea in the two translations is the same, as you can see: a man couldn't just abandon his sick wife, but needed to take care of her for the rest of her life, even if he married a second wife. But since 1955, when the translation on the left was first published, scholars have figured out that the Akkadian term originally translated as "fever" probably means "skin disease." So this was a pretty specific law. But they also figured out that the law didn't apply only to "seigniors" (high-ranking men), as the earlier translation suggested, but to all men. So it's always good to find a recent translation of an ancient text, because scholars are learning more and more all the time about what the ancient words mean.

By the way, a document that has been translated is still considered to be a primary source, even though the translator has interpreted what the text means. But you should be on the lookout for "paraphrased" or "retold" documents. These aren't primary sources at all, but documents that have been put into completely different words from those of the original. A paraphrase is quite different from a translation and often changes the meaning.

Some primary sources, including some in this book, don't reflect things that actually happened. Some are stories that the people of ancient times liked to hear from their parents or friends or professional storytellers, or that reflected ideas that they believed in. Often these stories are about gods and goddesses, heroes and heroines who performed superhuman feats. Historians use these primary sources not to learn about real events but to understand what the ancient people believed about themselves, their place in the universe, their gods, and their desires. For example, historians in the future won't read the Harry Potter books to learn about a real person named Harry Potter. They'll realize that he was imaginary. But they might learn something from the success of the books about how people of the early 21st century loved fantasy stories and wished they could somehow fight against evil forces just as Harry Potter does.

And now you are thinking like a historian. As you read the primary sources in this book, keep all these ideas and questions in mind. You won't be able to answer all the questions for each of the sources, but it's always helpful to think them through. Never trust a primary source to tell you the truth—it needs to be investigated and interpreted. In fact, this is a useful way of thinking about other things as well, not just historical documents. That ad on TV—does it have a particular audience in mind? Why was it produced? Can you trust it? That rumor you heard from a friend—was she an eyewitness or is she telling you something she heard from someone else?

Once you get used to analyzing primary sources, you will realize that ancient history (in fact, *any* history) is much more than a lot of facts to be memorized. It is a grand puzzle, full of fascinating characters, unsolved mysteries, surprising twists, and noisy disputes. The pieces of evidence, the primary sources, are your key to putting the puzzle together.

THE EARLY HUMAN WORLD

Writing was invented only about 5,000 years ago (and even then only in a few places on Earth), apparently tens of thousands of years after humans invented language. And hominids, ancient members of the human family, in turn had existed for millions of years before language was invented. Our primary sources for the vast span of time before writing began consist of objects found in excavations: bones, stone tools, art, weapons, and later the remains of buildings and pottery.

The best way for you to experience these primary sources is through the words of the people who uncovered them, the archaeologists and scientists who led excavations in all parts of the world to learn more about our really ancient past.

The book called *The Early Human World* includes many illustrations of the bones, tools, villages, and even whole preserved bodies that are mentioned in the excavators' descriptions.

1. Excitement Conquers the Flu

MARY LEAKEY, DISCLOSING THE PAST, PUBLISHED IN 1984, FINDS FROM 2 MILLION YEARS AGO

See chapter 6 in *The Early Human World*

Husband and wife archaeologists Louis and Mary Leakey worked together at Olduvai Gorge in Tanzania, Africa, for more than 20 years before they found their first hominid, an ancient member of the human family. Olduvai Gorge is only 300 feet deep, but the rocks at the bottom of the gorge were deposited there almost 2 million years ago. In their many seasons of working in the gorge, the Leakeys had discovered fossil animal bones and stone tools all the way from the bottom of the gorge up to the top. Yet they were still looking for the fossils of a creature able to make these tools on a day in July 1959 when Louis came down with the flu.

Archaeologists use numbers or letters, like **Bed I**, to keep track of the various areas being excavated or exposed. >

sediments, matter deposited by water >

FLK, an area at Olduvai with many levels of artifacts and fossils. >

These **thick** bones were unfamiliar to the experienced archaeologist Mary Leakey, so she doubted they could be hominid. >

in situ, Latin for "its original position" >

Then Louis got an attack of 'flu and retired to bed, and so it came about that on the morning of 17 July [1959] I went out by myself, with the two Dalmatians Sally and Victoria, to see what I could find of interest at nearby **Bed I** exposures [at Olduvai Gorge]. I turned my steps towards a site not far west of the junction of the two gorges [main and side gorges], where we knew that bones and stone artifacts were fairly common on the surface of Bed I **sediments**. The site was known as **FLK**. . . .

There was indeed plenty of material lying on the eroded surface at FLK, some no doubt as a result of the rains earlier that year. But one scrap of bone that caught and held my eye was not lying loose on the surface but projecting from beneath. It seemed to be part of a skull, including a mastoid process (the bony projection below the ear). It had a hominid look, but the bones seemed enormously thick —too **thick**, surely. I carefully brushed away a little of the deposit, and then I could see parts of two large teeth in place in the upper jaw. They *were* hominid. It was a hominid skull, apparently ***in situ***, and there was a lot of it there. I rushed back to camp to tell Louis, who leaped out of bed, and then we were soon back at the site, looking at my find together. Louis was sad that the skull was not of an early *Homo*, but he concealed his feelings well and expressed only mild disappointment. *'Zinjanthropus'* [*Australopithecus boisei*] had come into our lives.

After making this discovery, the Leakeys went on to find many more hominid remains in Olduvai Gorge. As it turned out, the hominid that Mary found in 1959 was probably not a toolmaker. An early species of our own genus, Homo, *was probably the maker of the tools.*

 Mary Leakey wrote two books about her work, *Olduvai Gorge: My Search for Early Man* (Collins, 1979) and *Disclosing the Past* (Doubleday, 1984). Two biographies are also available, *The Leakeys: Uncovering The Origins of Humankind,* by Margaret Poynter (Enslow, 1997), and *Mary Leakey: In Search of Human Beginnings,* by Deborah Heiligman (W. H. Freeman, 1995). *The Young Oxford Book of the Prehistoric World,* by Jill Bailey and Tony Seddon (Oxford University Press, 1999), discusses evolution, and *Wisdom of the Bones: In Search of Human Origins* (Vintage, 1997), by Alan Walker, gives the an account of the author's own discoveries of early hominids.

2. Rhinoceros for Dinner

“ RICK POTTS, DIARY, PUBLISHED IN 1999, FINDS FROM 780,000 YEARS AGO

See chapter 8 in *The Early Human World*

At Olorgesailie, an archaeological site about 45 miles southwest of Nairobi, the capital of Kenya, Africa, Rick Potts discovered a group of ancient rhinoceros bones and the stone tools that some of our ancestors may have used to make a meal of the animal. Potts and archaeologists from the Smithsonian Institution in Washington, D.C., have been excavating at Olorgesailie for a few weeks each year since 1985. Archaeologists have discovered stone tools and fossils dating to nearly a million years ago at this site, which was near a lake that sometimes dried out. One of our ancestors, Homo erectus, *probably made the stone tools that have been found here, though the archaeologists have not found any fossils belonging to this hominid at the site. This lack of fossils is not really surprising, because people rarely die at places they visit only briefly (which is true of most places visited by hunters and gatherers).*

One of the goals of the archaeologists' project was to find out what life was like for our early ancestors at Olorgesailie and how they coped when the climate and environment changed. When Potts and his team found animal bones, like those of this rhinoceros, and stone tools together on the site, they used them to find answers to several questions. For example, did Homo erectus *kill the rhino or did it just die of natural causes? Did* Homo erectus *use the tools to butcher the rhino so that the meat could be eaten there or somewhere else? Or were the stone tools left behind long before the rhino died at this spot?*

In his diary entry for July 16, 1999, Potts plays detective and tries to use the clues found at site B7/8-1—one particular area within the larger prehistoric site of Olorgesailie—to find out if Homo erectus *had rhino for dinner or not.*

in anatomical order, the bones of a skeleton lined up as they would have been in life, > showing they have not been disturbed or moved

indicative, evidence >

Site B7/8-1 certainly looks like a place where early humans butchered a large animal, probably a rhinoceros. We have about 25 bones from the animal, including some of the ribs and vertebrae arranged in roughly the correct **anatomical order**. This means that the excavations are right where the animal died (as a rhinoceros is too large to carry as one big mass, and transporting it in pieces would disturb the anatomical order). And we have sharp stone tools indicating the presence of humans at the site. All of the bones and tools are buried in a soil that is about 780,000 years old. Soils are **indicative** of stable land surfaces, so it wasn't a river, and the bones and tools were not simply washed together from different places. All of the bones and artifacts were found in the top layer of the soil, so perhaps the objects that remained on the surface gradually sank into the soil whenever it became soggy. . . .

But what could be wrong with our picture of this site? The interesting puzzles are in the details, and the details of this excavation pose some good challenges. For one thing, the stone artifacts lifted from the site today were taken from below the deepest extent of the bones. How did the animal get on top of the tools? Could it be that a rhinoceros 780,000 years ago just happened to keel over right on top of some stone tool flakes left behind by early humans, maybe left there after sharpening sticks to dig for roots and tubers?

Fossil bones crack under the weight of soil. Roots of plants often **exploit the** > **cracks,** meaning they grow through the cracks, making them wider.

artifacts, objects made by humans >

For another thing, we have found evidence that modern plants and animals have also altered the original ancient soil. Modern roots are found throughout the site; many **exploit the cracks** in the fossil bones, and we have found both live burrowing insects, and egg cases within the fossil-artifact layer. The fact that present day roots and burrowing insects are found in an ancient soil containing fossils and stone tools is a complicating factor! Yet this could explain why some of the **artifacts** were found as much as 20 centimeters below (and above) the bones of the animal. They could have been repositioned through time as modern plants and animals churn the sediments. . . . So maybe the tools and the rhino were associated after all, in the original condition of the site.

In doing research like this, it is important to keep observing the details, and to keep asking questions. At Site B7/8-1, we need more clues. We'll extend the excavation later on.

The website of the Olorgesailie excavation (www.mnh.si.edu/anthro/humanorigins/aop/olorg1999/index.htm) includes lots of information and photographs of the site. *Fossil Trail: How We Know What We Think We Know about Human Evolution*, by Ian Tattersall (Oxford University Press, 1997), includes information about human evolution and the discoveries that have helped us understand it.

3. A Neolithic Village

ANDREW MOORE, "A PRE-NEOLITHIC FARMERS' VILLAGE ON THE EUPHRATES," PUBLISHED IN 1979, FINDS FROM 9,000 YEARS AGO

Archaeologist Andrew Moore was in charge of excavating Abu Hureyra in northern Syria before it was flooded by the waters of a reservoir that formed behind a dam built in 1973. Stone Age (Neolithic) farmers lived at Abu Hureyra about 9,000 years ago, growing wheat, barley, and other crops and, a little later, herding some of the world's first domesticated sheep and goats. As a result of careful excavation, Moore was able to tell us what the village of Abu Hureyra looked like 9,000 years ago.

See chapter 19 in *The Early Human World*

What did Neolithic Abu Hureyra look like? Its numerous **rectilinear** houses were built close together, with only narrow lanes and little courts between them. Each house, made of mud brick, consisted of several small rooms connected by doorways; some of the doorways were conventional but others had very high sills. Many rooms had **burnished** plaster floors that were colored black and occasionally had red **schematic motifs**. The walls of the houses were given a coat of whitewash. It seems likely that each house was occupied by one family.

< **rectilinear,** formed by straight lines

< **burnished,** rubbed to make shiny

< **schematic motifs,** designs that are repeated in a particular pattern

In addition to Andrew Moore's article, from which this description of Abu Hureyra comes, other *Scientific American* articles about Abu Hureyra include "Gazelle Killing in Stone Age Syria," by A. J. Legge and P. A. Rowley-Conwy (*Scientific American* 255 (8):88–95, August 1987) and "The Eloquent Bones of Abu Hureyra," by T. Molleson (*Scientific American* 271 (2):70–75, August 1994). The Eyewitness Books volume *The Early Humans,* by Philip Wilkinson (Knopf, 1989), mentions early farming villages like Abu Hureyra.

4. Preserving the Past for the Future

FRANK G. MATERO, "THE LOST CITY OF ÇATALHÖYÜK" AND "PRESERVING THE EXCAVATED PAST," PUBLISHED IN 2002, FINDS FROM 9,000 YEARS AGO

See chapter 20 in *The Early Human World*

In the 1960s, one of the most important excavations in the Near East was at the site of Çatalhöyük in Turkey. The excavators found a town from almost 9,000 years ago, where the houses were built right next to one another, with no streets between them. People had entered their houses from the roofs. The paintings on the walls of the houses, of patterns, animals, hunts, and other scenes, were unlike anything that had been found at any other site. Unfortunately, though, many of the wall paintings disintegrated rapidly once they had been excavated.

So when excavations at Çatalhöyük began again in the 1990s, one of the top priorities of the excavation team was conservation. They wanted to make sure that this time the evidence wasn't lost as soon as it was exposed to the air. Frank Matero, a conservator at the site, explains his work.

If you visit the site today, you will see one mud-brick house with all its white sculpted plasters preserved under a big canvas shelter designed to protect and display the building to visitors. This ancient house has many recognizable features including food bins made from mud walls, cooking and heating fireplaces, low doors for passage between rooms, and even the scars of a ladder that was embedded in the wall from the roof entrance above. . . . In some rooms, the floors were colored red and walls brilliant white with horizontal sculpted ridges for decoration . . .

Techniques [for preserving the architecture, mural paintings, and sculpture] include stabilizing a structure in its original place, removing parts of the structure, and lifting and transporting the entire structure off-site using a special **rig** developed specifically for this purpose. . . . Rooms that will be preserved in place will need to be conserved and covered with shelters for protection from the wind, rain, and snow.

< **rig,** machine

To develop treatments for the preservation of the mural paintings and sculptures, conservators re-created the materials and techniques used to create the ancient works of art in the laboratory. These replicas were then allowed to deteriorate so that conservation treatments could be tested on them before being applied to the ancient artworks.

Several new conservation treatments are being used on the earthen buildings, wall paintings, and sculpture. Among these is injecting **liquid mortar grout** into the walls to reattach falling plasters and cracked mud brick. **Salts** that have formed on the surfaces of the walls over hundreds of years are removed with scalpels and sponges. Because the ancient artwork is the most important aspect to be preserved, painting over the mural is never done.

liquid mortar grout, a liquid plasterlike substance used to fill < cracks or spaces

< Naturally occurring **salts** in soil and mud brick tend to come to the surface over time, often damaging that surface.

The whole March/April 2002 issue of *Dig* magazine is dedicated to the excavations at Çatalhöyük, with articles by the excavator, conservator, and other specialists. Farming communities like Çatalhöyük are explored in *Ancient Agriculture: From Foraging to Farming,* by Michael and Mary B. Woods (Lerner Publishing, 2000). "Conservation for Kids" is the name of a website that gives interesting examples of conservation projects (www.artlab.sa.gov.au/features/cfk/index.asp).

5. A Frozen Stiff

“ **KONRAD SPINDLER, THE MAN IN THE ICE, PUBLISHED IN 1994, REMAINS FROM 5,300 YEARS AGO**

Erika and Helmut Simon were on vacation hiking high in the Alps when they discovered the body of the Iceman in September 1991 as it emerged from the melting ice of a glacier. At first, nobody realized that the Iceman, who came to be known as Ötzi, had died long ago. In fact, he died about 5,300 years ago, and his body was preserved by being frozen in the ice. He is the first prehistoric human to be found

See chapter 21 in *The Early Human World*

with his clothing and equipment. He died after being shot in the back with an arrow tipped with a flint arrowhead. Nobody bothered to bury him or take away his possessions, so there they stayed until the Simons found him thousands of years later. Archaeologists have learned an enormous amount about the Iceman's life by studying his body and his equipment.

This account of the discovery was written by Konrad Spindler, the leader of an international team of scientists who studied the Iceman.

Later Helmut Simon would describe their discovery to us like this: "From a distance of 8 or 10 meters we suddenly saw something brown sticking out of the ice. Our first thought was that it was rubbish, perhaps a doll, because by now there is plenty of litter even in the high mountains. As we came closer, Erika said: 'But it's a man!'". . . .

Sticking out of the ice is a leather-brown round bald skull with a medallion-sized injury. Also visible are the shoulders and back, draped against a rock. The face is immersed in water, with dirt around the chin. The arms cannot be seen and seem to be missing. Because of its delicate proportions, Erika suggests that it is the body of a woman.

"We thought it was a mountaineer who died here. We were shocked and didn't touch the body. There was a blue ski-clip lying nearby, the rubber strap used for tying skis for transport. We thought the accident probably happened ten or twenty years ago. Not far from the body we saw a piece of birch bark, which used to be a tube but had been squashed flat, wound round with string or leather and open at both ends. Helmut picked it up, looked at it carefully and put it back. We memorized the exact position of the body before we left. Helmut took a photograph as a record, in case the place couldn't be found again from our description."

It was the last frame of his film—the photograph of the year.

Many books have been written about the Iceman, for readers of all ages. They include *Ice Mummy,* by M. and C. E. Dubowski (Random House, 1998); *Frozen Man,* by D. Getz and P. McCarty (Henry Holt, 1996); and *Discovering the Iceman,* by Shelley Tanaka (Hyperion, 1996). Scientist Konrad Spindler wrote the book from which the source is taken: *The Man in the Ice: The Discovery of a 5,000-Year-Old Body Reveals the Secrets of the Stone Age* (Harmony, 1994).

6. A Native American Time Capsule

RICHARD DAUGHERTY AND RUTH KIRK, "OZETTE, WASHINGTON," PUBLISHED IN 1996, FINDS FROM 500 YEARS AGO

See chapter 24 in *The Early Human World*

Most archaeologists spend their entire careers without ever finding an ancient basket or wooden canoe paddle. Basketry and wood survive for a long time only under very unusual conditions, either very dry or, as in this case, very wet. Richard Daugherty was one lucky archaeologist to have the opportunity to excavate this 500-year-old house at a site called Ozette on the Pacific coast of Washington State. He must have been very excited about digging this site, but he had to hurry because people had begun to steal the artifacts that had been exposed by storm waves. The artifacts belong to the Makah Indian Nation, who still live in this region at the northwestern tip of the United States. The Makah, who hunted whales for centuries, still get much of their food and income from the sea.

Three years passed, and the calendar showed February 1970, when Daugherty received a phone call urging him back to Ozette. It came from Ed Claplanhoo, chairman of the Makah Tribal Council at the time and formerly a student at Washington State University. Storm waves driven high onto the beach had undercut the bank at Ozette, Claplanhoo reported, and wet **midden** had slumped. Deep layers within the bank now were exposed, and old-style fish-hooks of wood and bone, parts of **inlaid** boxes, and a canoe paddle had washed out from where they had lain buried for centuries. Hikers had found the artifacts. They were even carrying them away—and once such items are gathered up and taken off by collectors, they no longer reveal the life of the people who made them and used them. They become mere things.

< **midden,** trash heap

< **inlaid,** having material, such as different colored wood or shell, set in the surface to make a pattern

Daugherty listened to the tribal chairman's full account; then he headed almost straight from the phone to his car. He had to get to the coast and see for himself. If the discoveries were as important as they sounded, he would need to raise finances, hire a crew, round up the necessary field equipment, and begin excavating as soon as possible. . . .

The slumped bank was about five meters high. Wild crabapple trees, elderberry, and sword ferns had slid with the mud and now formed a junglelike tangle. Daugherty climbed in among the roots and limbs, sinking over his boot tops in the ooze. His eye lit on planks that were sticking out end on, and a basketry rain hat of the kind women twined from spruce roots in the **old days**. There were also bone points used for shooting birds, halibut hooks, a harpoon shaft, and part of a carved wooden box.

old days, when the community at Ozette was flourishing, around 500 years ago

Daugherty felt a familiar excitement. If this much had been brought to the surface, what must still lie hidden? . . .

The project was like opening a time capsule. Here was an Indian home from the time before Columbus set sail for America. Everything was present—sleeping benches, cooking hearths, storage boxes, harpoons, bows and arrows, baskets, mats, tool kits. All the household possessions of a family of whale hunters—and all of it tossed into a muddy jumble. The crew's job was to untangle the mess and discover its meaning. Find the roof planks and distinguish them from the wall planks. Hose away more of the mud slide and locate the north end of the house (so far work had been only in the south end). Keep notes and make drawings and photographs. Preserve each piece as it was lifted from the mud—the splintered boards the house was built of, the wooden bowls that once held seal oil and whale oil, the mussel-shell lance blades, the elk-antler wedges—everything.

Ruth Kirk describes the archaeological expedition in *Hunters of the Whale: An Adventure of Northwest Coast Archaeology* (William Morrow, 1974). Two books that include legends of Native Americans of the Pacific Northwest are *Spirit of the Cedar People* (DK Publishing, 1998) and *Echoes of the Elders* (DK Publishing, 1997), both by Chief Lelooska and Christine Normandin.

THE ANCIENT NEAR EASTERN WORLD

Mesopotamians wrote on clay tablets using a reed stylus that impressed the wedge-shaped signs, called cuneiform, into the clay. Mesopotamian scribes first used writing only for keeping track of workers and taxes, but gradually they found new uses for this wonderful invention: royal proclamations, legal contracts, personal letters, hymns, poems, stories, and much more.

Clay survives well in the ground, so hundreds of thousands of documents have been found from ancient Near Eastern civilizations. Although the Israelites used papyrus, a writing surface made from reeds, which falls apart, the Hebrew Bible survives in many handwritten copies from later times.

In addition to the texts reproduced here, a wide variety of primary sources can be found in the book *The Ancient Near Eastern World,* including more excerpts from the Hebrew Bible such as the creation story, the tale of David and Goliath, and the Ten Commandments.

7. A Fearsome Goddess

ENHEDUANNA, "THE ADORATION OF INANNA IN UR," 24TH OR 23RD CENTURY BCE

See chapters 5 and 9 of *The Ancient Near Eastern World*

This hymn shows how Mesopotamians praised their gods, exalting each one and telling that god that he or she was the greatest of all. It portrays Inanna as a war goddess, known for destroying her enemies.

The author, the priestess Enheduanna, was the daughter of King Sargon of Akkad and was the first-known author in history to take credit for her writing. All previous authors had been anonymous, because the Mesopotamians thought the written texts were more important than the names of the people who wrote them. Enheduanna was a priestess of the moon god Nanna (also known as Sin), and she emphasizes here that her hymn is not to Nanna but to Inanna. Elsewhere in the hymn, she tells Nanna not to be troubled by this.

In the . . . battle, everything was struck down before you,
My queen, you are all devouring in your power,
You kept on attacking like an attacking storm,
Kept on blowing (louder) than the howling storm. . . .
My queen . . . the great gods,
Fled before you like fluttering bats,
Could not stand before your awesome face,
Could not approach your awesome forehead.
Who can soothe your angry heart! . . .
Queen, **paramount** in the land, who has (ever) paid you
(enough) **homage**! . . .

paramount, superior to all others

homage, flattering attention

The kingship of heaven has been seized by the woman
Inanna,
At whose feet lies the flood-land.
That woman [Inanna] so exalted, who has made me tremble,
together with the city of **Ur,**
Stay her, let her heart be soothed by me. . . .

Ur, a large city in southern Mesopotamia, where Enheduanna lived

"You are known, you are known"—it is not of Nanna
that I have recited it, it is of you that I have recited it.
"You are known by your heaven-like height,

You are known by your earth-like breadth,
You are known by your destruction of rebel-lands,
You are known by your massacring their people,
You are known by your devouring their dead like a dog,
You are known by your fierce **countenance**.
. . . You are known by your flashing eyes.
. . . You are known by your many triumphs"—
It is not of Nanna that I have recited it, it is of you that
I have recited it.

< **countenance,** face, especially facial expression

Benjamin Foster's two-volume set *Before the Muses* (2nd ed., CDL Press, 1996) includes translations of many hymns and works of literature from Mesopotamia. Inanna is also a main character in the story *The City of Rainbows: A Tale from Ancient Sumer,* retold by Karen Foster (University Museum, University of Pennsylvania, 1999). This book includes pictures based on ancient Sumerian mosaics.

8. What Did You Do in School?

A SCRIBE'S EXERCISE, "SCHOOLDAYS," ABOUT 2000 BCE

In answer to the question, "What did you do in school?" a Mesopotamian schoolboy describes his day. We can see that it was a day school (he lived at home), that discipline was strict, and that the lessons were made up almost entirely of practicing writing on clay tablets. Although children were required to speak Sumerian at school (and this exercise was written in Sumerian), it was not spoken in most homes by this time. Akkadian had become the spoken language of Mesopotamia. At the beginning of this section, the boy is growing tired of school, but the description ends with the teacher telling the boy that he is a good student and will benefit from his education. This text was used as a writing assignment for boys in schools for scribes.

See chapter 14 of *The Ancient Near Eastern World*

I recited my tablet, ate my lunch, prepared my (new) tablet, wrote it, finished it; then my model tablets were brought to me; and in the afternoon my exercise tablets were brought to me. . . .

My headmaster read my tablet and said: "There is something missing." He **caned** me. . . .

caned, beat with a < stick

The fellow in charge of silence said: "Why did you talk without permission?" He caned me. . . .

The fellow in charge of Sumerian said: "Why didn't you speak Sumerian?" He caned me.

My teacher said: "Your handwriting is unsatisfactory." He caned me. (And so) I (began to) hate the scribal art, (began to) neglect the scribal art. . . .

The teacher was brought from school, and after entering in the house, he was seated on the "big chair." The schoolboy attended and served him, and whatever he learned of the scribal art, he unfolded to his father. Then did the father in the joy of his heart say joyfully to the headmaster of the school: "My little fellow has opened (wide) his hand, (and) you have made wisdom enter there; you showed him all the fine points of the scribal art; you made him see solutions of the mathematical and arithmetical (problems). . . . "

(The teacher said:) "Young fellow, (because) you hated not my words, neglected them not, (may you) complete the scribal art from beginning to end."

The full text of this story, along with several other Mesopotamian compositions about school life, is in Samuel N. Kramer's *The Sumerians* (University of Chicago Press, 1963) in the chapter titled "Education: The Sumerian School." Mathematics, which was taught in Mesopotamian schools, is featured in a book called *Science in Ancient Mesopotamia*, by Carol Moss (Franklin Watts, 1998).

9. "Enjoy Yourself Always"

EPIC OF GILGAMESH, 18TH OR 17TH CENTURY BCE

See chapter 7 of *The Ancient Near Eastern World*

The Epic of Gilgamesh *is the earliest known epic poem from any civilization. An epic is a long poem that tells the story of a hero's adventures. Gilgamesh was a king of the city of Uruk who had great adventures with his friend Enkidu. After Enkidu died, Gilgamesh decided that he did not want to die and went off in search of eternal life. The epic includes some universal themes that people have thought about for centuries, including friendship, adventure, the purpose of life, and the finality of death.*

In this section, which is found in an early form of the epic (but not in the well-known 12th-century-BCE version), Gilgamesh is distraught over the death of Enkidu. He begins his search for eternal life and comes across a tavern keeper named Siduri. She advises Gilgamesh not to try to seek immortality, which is reserved for the gods, but to enjoy a simple life.

"O tavern-keeper, I have looked on your face,
But I would not meet death, that I fear so much."
Said the tavern-keeper to him, to Gilgamesh:
"O Gilgamesh, where are you wandering?

"The life that you seek you never will find:
when the gods created mankind,
death they **dispensed** to mankind,
life they kept for themselves.

< **dispensed**, gave out

"But you, Gilgamesh, let your belly be full,
enjoy yourself always by day and by night!
Make merry each day,
Dance and play day and night!

"Let your clothes be clean,
let your head be washed, may you bathe in water!
Gaze on the child who holds your hand,
Let your wife enjoy your repeated embrace!

"For such is the destiny of mortal men."

A three-volume set of picture books by Ludmilla Zeman, *Gilgamesh the King, The Revenge of Ishtar,* and *The Last Quest of Gilgamesh* (Tundra Books, 1998), offers a good version of the Gilgamesh epic. The story is slightly different from the original and the illustrations in the first book include art styles, fashions, and architecture from the third millennium BCE and the first millennium BCE mixed together. Another recent version of the epic is *Gilgamesh the Hero,* by Geraldine McCaughrean (Eerdmans, 2002), which has a longer, more accurate version of the story with fewer pictures.

10. Rules for a Just Society

HAMMURABI'S LAWS, ABOUT 1755 BCE

See chapters 10 and 11 of *The Ancient Near Eastern World*

When King Hammurabi of Babylon proclaimed his collection of laws, late in his reign, he emphasized that he had created them in order to protect people in society who were seen as weak, such as widows and orphans. Laws 2 and 3 show how important it was for witnesses to tell the truth. Laws 22 and 23 are about robbery. When the victim was supposed to describe his lost property "before the god," this meant swearing an oath about what had been stolen. Whether or not the robber was found, the victim still had a right to have the stolen goods replaced. Law 53 is typical of many laws in the collection that have to do with agriculture—it determines who is responsible for damage to crops. Laws 138 and 148 concern marriage and divorce. Law 168 is about fathers and sons. Law 278 governs the purchase of a slave who has epilepsy, a disease that the Mesopotamians believed was sent by the gods.

capital offense, a most serious crime, punishable by death >

Law 3. If a man comes forward to give false testimony in a case but cannot bring evidence for his accusation, if that case involves a **capital offense**, that man shall be killed.

Law 4. If he comes forward to give false testimony for a case whose penalty is grain or silver, he shall be assessed the penalty for that case.

Law 22. If a man commits a robbery and is then seized, that man shall be killed.

Law 23. If the robber should not be seized, the man who has been robbed shall establish the extent of his lost property before the god; and the city and the governor in whose territory and district the robbery was committed shall replace his lost property to him.

Law 53. If a man neglects to reinforce the embankment of the irrigation canal of his field and does not reinforce its embankment, and then a breach opens in its embankment and allows the water to carry away the common irrigated area, the man in whose embankment the breach opened shall replace the grain whose loss he caused.

A **first-ranking wife,** the first wife a man has married or, if he has more than one wife, the most important one >

Law 138. If a man intends to divorce his **first-ranking wife** who did not bear him children, he shall give her silver as much as was her **bridewealth** and restore to her the dowry that she brought from her father's house, and he shall divorce her.

< **bridewealth,** the goods or silver that a new husband gives his fiancée's family as a gesture of goodwill.

Law 148. if a man marries a woman and later a skin disease seizes her and he decides to marry another woman, he will not divorce his wife whom the skin disease seized; she shall reside in quarters he constructs and he shall continue to support her as long as she lives.

Law 168. If a man should decide to **disinherit** his son and declares to the judges, "I will disinherit my son," the judges shall investigate his case and if the son is not guilty of a **grave** offense deserving the penalty of disinheritance, the father may not disinherit his son.

< **disinherit,** prevent someone from inheriting

< **grave,** serious

Law 278. If a man purchases a slave or slave woman and within his one-month period epilepsy then befalls him [the slave], he shall return him to his seller and the buyer shall take back the silver that he weighed and delivered.

Epilogue: These are the just decisions which Hammurabi, the able king, has established.... In order that the mighty not wrong the weak, to provide just ways for the orphan and the widow, I have inscribed my precious pronouncements upon my **stela** and set it up before the statue of me, the king of justice, in the city of Babylon.... Let any wronged man who has a lawsuit come before the statue of me, the king of justice, and let him have my inscribed stela read aloud to him, thus may he hear my precious pronouncements and let my stela reveal the lawsuit for him; may he examine his case, may he calm his troubled heart, and may he praise me...

< **stela,** carved stone pillar or slab

The full text of Hammurabi's laws is found in Martha Roth's *Law Collections from Mesopotamia and Asia Minor* (Scholars Press, 1997), along with translations of other collections of laws. The book also includes a version of the laws in the original ancient language of Akkadian (using modern letters, not cuneiform), so readers can get a sense of how the ancient language sounded.

11. "You Do Not Love Me"

BABYLONIAN LETTER, ABOUT 1900–1700 BCE

See chapters 13 and 14 of *The Ancient Near Eastern World*

This letter from a boy to his mother gives us a glimpse into everyday life in Mesopotamia around the time of Hammurabi: the boy, living away from home (it's unclear why), needs some new clothes, and he finds various ways to make his mother feel guilty for not sending them. We see that the mother is in charge of the household budget and that the boy's status is based, at least in part, on appearing to be wealthy. The letter starts with the words, "Tell the lady," because the boy dictated his letter to a scribe, and the scribe was writing directions for another scribe who would read the letter to the boy's mother. The scribe wrote the letter out on a small clay tablet. Almost all letters at this time began with the hope that the gods would bless the recipient with good health.

Tell the Lady Zinu: Iddin-Sin sends the following message:

May the gods Shamash, Marduk, and Ilabrat keep you forever in good health for my sake.

From year to year, the clothes of the young gentlemen here become better, but you let my clothes get worse from year to year. Indeed, you persisted in making my clothes poorer and more scanty. At a time when in our house wool is used up like bread, you have made me poor clothes. The son of Adad-iddinam, whose father is only an assistant of my father, has two new sets of clothes, while you fuss even about a single set of clothes for me. In spite of the fact that you bore me and his mother only adopted him, his mother loves him, while you, you do not love me!

A. Leo Oppenheim's *Letters from Mesopotamia* (University of Chicago Press, 1967) includes many letters about aspects of life in the ancient Near East—some of them, like this one, from ordinary people, some from kings and governors.

12. Brothers Who Never Met

AMARNA LETTER, FROM KING TUSHRATTA TO KING AMENHOTEP III, ABOUT 1355 BCE

See chapter 17 of *The Ancient Near Eastern World*

The kings of Egypt, Mittani (now Syria), Babylonia (now Iraq), Hatti (now Turkey), and Alashiya (now Cyprus) wrote to one another regularly during the reign of the Egyptian king Amenhotep III (who was also known as Nimmureya), each calling one another "brother" to show that they were equal in importance. But they had other, real relationships to one another as well, because the kings married one another's daughters and sisters. Tushratta, king of Mittani, could call himself father-in-law of Amenhotep III because his daughter was married to the Egyptian king. As the following letter shows the kings wished one another well, hoped that their daughters would have happy marriages to the foreign kings, and sent messengers, letters, and gifts back and forth between their countries. They also prayed that the gods of both their countries would watch over them. But the kings themselves never met in person—it would have been too risky to leave home for a journey of many weeks to another country.

Say to Nimmureya, Great King, king of Egypt, my brother, my son-in-law, whom I love and who loves me: Thus Tushratta, Great King, the king of Mittani, your brother, your father-in-law, and one who loves you. For me all goes well. For my brother and my son-in-law, may all go well. For your household, for your wives, for your sons, for your men, for your chariots, for your horses, for your country, and for whatever else belongs to you, may all go very well.

I have given [you] my daughter to be the wife of my brother, whom I love. May [the gods] Shimige and Shaushka go before her. May they make her the image of my brother's desire. May my brother rejoice on that day. May Shimige and Shaushka grant my brother a great blessing, exquisite joy. May they bless him and may you, my brother, live forever.

Mane, my brother's messenger, and Hane, my brother's interpreter, I have exalted like gods. I have given them many presents and treated them very kindly, for their report was excellent. In every thing about them, I have never seen men with such an appearance. May my gods and the gods of my brother protect them.

I herewith dispatch to my brother [my messenger] Nahram-ashshi..., and I send 1 **maninnu**-necklace of genuine lapis-lazuli and gold as the greeting-gift of my brother. May it rest on the neck of my brother for 100,000 years.

maninnu, an Akkadian term for a particular style

William L. Moran includes translations in *The Amarna Letters* (Johns Hopkins University Press, 1992) of all the letters that were found at Amarna, Egypt, from the reigns of Amenhotep III and his son, Akhenaten. Joann Fletcher's book *Chronicle of a Pharaoh: The Intimate Life of Amenhotep III* (Oxford University Press, 2000) gives a vivid description of the Egyptian king's opulent life.

13. Adam and Eve Tricked by the Serpent

THE BOOK OF GENESIS, THE HEBREW BIBLE

See chapter 20 of *The Ancient Near Eastern World*

The Book of Genesis in the Hebrew Bible describes what the Israelites believed about how God had created man and woman. The names of this first couple are usually given as Adam and Eve, though Adam simply means "man" in Hebrew. Eve's name comes from a Hebrew word meaning "life."

In the day that the Lord God made the earth and the heavens, when no plant of the field was yet in the earth and no herb of the field had yet sprung up... then the Lord God formed man from the dust of the ground, and breathed into his nostrils the breath of life; and the man became a living being. And the Lord God planted a garden in Eden, in the east; and there he put the man whom he had formed. Out of the ground the Lord God made to grow every tree that is pleasant to the sight and good for food, the tree of life also in the midst of the garden, and the tree of the knowledge of good and evil....

The Lord God took the man and put him in the garden of Eden to till it and keep it. And the Lord God commanded the man, "You may freely eat of every tree of the garden; but of the tree of the knowledge of good and evil you shall not eat, for in the day that you eat of it you shall die...."

Then the Lord God said, "It is not good that the man should be alone; I will make him a helper as his partner."... So the Lord God caused a deep sleep to fall upon the man, and he slept; then he took one of his ribs and closed up its place with flesh. And the rib that the Lord God had taken from the man he made into a woman and brought her to the man....

Now the serpent was more crafty than any other wild animal that the Lord God had made. He said to the woman, "Did God say, 'You shall not eat of the fruit of the tree that is in the middle of the garden, nor shall you touch it, or you shall die.'" But the serpent said to the woman, "You will not die; for God knows that when you eat of it your eyes will be opened, and you will be like God, knowing good and evil." So... she took of its fruit and ate; and she also gave some to her husband, who was with her and he ate....

Then the Lord God said to the woman, "What is this that you have done?" The woman said "The serpent tricked me, and I ate." ...

Then the Lord God said, "See, the man has become like one of us, knowing good and evil; and now, he might reach out his hand and take also from the tree of life, and eat, and live forever"—therefore the Lord God sent him forth from the garden of Eden, to till the ground from which he was taken.

Fran Manushkin's book *Daughters of Fire: Heroines of the Bible* (Harcourt, 2001) has a section on Eve, the first woman in the Biblical creation story, and includes studies of many other Biblical women.

14. A Successful Commander and a Jealous King

THE FIRST BOOK OF SAMUEL, THE HEBREW BIBLE

When Saul was king of Israel, his military commander, David (who was also a court musician), achieved many successes in battle against Israel's enemies, the Philistines, and became increasingly popular with the Israelite people. The Biblical authors describe Saul as very jealous of David's success and popularity. After Saul's death, David became king of Israel. Throughout the Hebrew Bible, as here, success is seen as a sign of God's support.

See chapter 18 of *The Ancient Near Eastern World*

As they were coming home, when David returned from killing the Philistine, the women came out of all the towns of Israel, singing and dancing, to meet King Saul, with tambourines, with songs of joy, and with musical instruments. And the women sang to one another as they made merry,

> "Saul has killed his thousands,
> and David his ten thousands."

Saul was very angry, for this saying displeased him. He said, "They have ascribed to David ten thousands, and to me they have ascribed thousands; what more can he have but the kingdom?" So Saul eyed David from that day on.

The next day an evil spirit from God rushed upon Saul and he raved within his house, while David was playing the lyre, as he did day by day. Saul had his spear in his hand; and Saul threw the spear, for he thought, "I will pin David to the wall." But David eluded him twice.

Saul was afraid of David, because the Lord was with him but had departed from Saul. So Saul removed him from his presence, and made him a commander of a thousand; and David marched out and came in, leading the army. David had success in all his undertakings; for the Lord was with him. When Saul saw that he had great success, he stood in awe of him. But all Israel and Judah loved David; for it was he who marched out and came in leading them.

David, by Barbara Cohen (Houghton Mifflin, 1995), is a biography of the Israelite king based on the Biblical tales as well as archaeological finds.

15. Reducing Babylon to Dust

SENNACHERIB, ROYAL INSCRIPTION, ABOUT 685 BCE

See chapter 21 of *The Ancient Near Eastern World*

The Assyrian empire dominated the entire Near East in the eighth and seventh centuries BCE. *Sennacherib, like all the Assyrian kings, wrote many royal inscriptions boasting about his great achievements. Unlike earlier kings, he devoted more energy to administering his empire—especially to finding ways to bring more water to farms—*

than he did to military campaigns. His major, and unpopular, military achievement was the conquest and destruction of Babylon. In this inscription, he starts by describing himself as an all-powerful warrior and provider for his people. His description of his conquest of Babylon must have worried the Assyrians as well as their rivals, the Babylonians, since smashing statues of gods was always an unwise thing to do. The Assyrians believed in the power of the Babylonian gods and must have feared their anger. But the next Assyrian king, Sennacherib's son, Esarhaddon, soon rebuilt Babylon.

Sennacherib, the great king, the mighty king, king of the universe, king of Assyria, king of the four quarters (of the world), ruler of widespreading peoples... maker of Assyria, who completes its **metropolis; subduer** of the enemies' land, destroyer of their towns; who digs canals, opens wells, runs irrigation ditches, who brings plenty and abundance to the wide acres of Assyria... the support of his land, exalted in battle and warfare, the protecting shadow of his armies, am I....

< **metropolis,** city; **subduer,** conqueror

After I had destroyed Babylon, had smashed the gods thereof, and had struck down its people with the sword,—that the ground of that city might be carried off, I removed its ground and had it carried to the Euphrates (and on) to the sea. Its earth was carried unto **Dilmun**. The Dilmunites saw it, and the terror of the fear of [the god] Assur fell upon them and they brought their treasures. With their treasures they sent **artisans,** mustered from their land,... a copper chariot, copper tools, vessels of the workmanship of their land,—at the destruction of Babylon.

< **Dilmun,** island in the Persian Gulf

< **artisans,** craftspeople

To quiet the heart of Assur, my lord, that people should bow in submission before his exalted might, I removed the dust of Babylon for presents to (the most) distant peoples.

Step into Mesopotamia, by Lorna Oakes (Lorenz, 2001), includes several sections on the Assyrians: "An Important City," "Running the Empire," "Fighting Forces," "Palace Builders," "Furnishing the Palace," "The Lion Hunt of the King," and "Royal Libraries and Museums."

16. "Flies Enter an Open Mouth"

MESOPOTAMIAN PROVERBS, SECOND AND FIRST MILLENNIUMS BCE, AND THE BOOK OF PROVERBS, THE HEBREW BIBLE

See chapters 12, 13, and 20 of *The Ancient Near Eastern World*

These sayings reflect folk wisdom in the Mesopotamian civilization. They show the emphasis on the importance of honesty, hard work, kindness, moderation, and restraint. Scribes collected and recorded Mesopotamian proverbs on clay tablets.

Justice and law

He who despises a just decision, who loves evil decisions, is an **abomination** to (the god) Shamash.

abomination, > something disgusting

To accept a verdict is possible. To accept a curse is impossible.

Wealth

To be wealthy and demand more is an abomination to the god.

He who possesses many things is constantly on guard.

Family

Marrying is human. Getting children is divine.

One who does not support a wife, who does not support a son, is a dishonest person who does not support himself.

Work

Those who get excited should not become **foremen**. A shepherd should not become a farmer.

foremen, > managers

The strong man makes his living by the work of his arms, but the weak man by selling his children [into slavery].

Being a good person

Let kindness be repaid to him who repays a kindness.

Being strong does not compare to having intelligence.

Who compares with someone who has humility? Well-being comes with it.

He who insults is insulted. He who sneers is sneered at.

Flies enter an open mouth.

The Bible includes many proverbs that are similar to the Mesopotamian ones. They are collected in the Hebrew Bible's Book of Proverbs.

Justice and law

Whoever says to the wicked, "You are innocent" will be cursed by peoples, abhorred by nations; but those who rebuke the wicked will have delight.

Wealth

Whoever gives to the poor will lack nothing, but one who turns a blind eye will get many a curse.

A good name is to be chosen rather than great riches, and favor is better than silver or gold.

Family

A child who loves wisdom makes a parent glad

Listen to your father who begot you, and do not despise your mother when she is old.

Work

The lazy person does not plow in season; harvest comes, and there is nothing to be found.

A slack hand causes poverty, but the hand of the diligent makes rich.

Being a good person

Fools show their anger at once, but the **prudent** ignore an insult. <**prudent,** cautious

The lips of the wise spread knowledge, not so the minds of fools.

Pride goes before destruction and a **haughty** spirit before a fall. <**haughty,** proud

Let another praise you and not your own mouth.

Bible Lands, by Jonathan Tubb (Eyewitness Books, Knopf, 1991) includes plenty of information about daily life among the Israelites and other ancient Near Eastern peoples.

THE ANCIENT EGYPTIAN WORLD

The ancient Egyptian scribes used hieroglyphic writing—beautiful, elaborate little pictures of people, animals, and symbols—to record important texts on the stone walls of tombs and monuments. They also used a simpler, cursive form of writing called hieratic for writing on papyrus.

Inscriptions on stone survive well in any climate. Papyrus tends to disintegrate, especially when it gets wet. The damp earth of the Nile River valley destroyed most ancient Egyptian papyrus documents long ago. But papyrus that was left in the desert survived just fine. Since the Egyptians buried their dead in the deserts, most of the preserved papyri are from tombs.

The book called *The Ancient Egyptian World* includes not only more Egyptian documents but also descriptions of Egypt written by ancient Greek authors, such as Diodorus Siculus and Herodotus.

17. How to Get Ahead at Court

THE MAXIMS OF PTAH-HOTEP, 20TH CENTURY BCE

See chapter 8 in *The Ancient Egyptian World*

If you were an Egyptian leader, someone working in the king's court, how should you behave? Someone, supposedly the high-ranking Vizier Ptah-hotep, wrote a book of etiquette giving detailed instructions, called maxims, on proper manners for members of the nobility and upper class. Ptah-hotep lived during the Old Kingdom period, from 2715 to 2170 BCE*, which Egyptians saw as a golden age of their culture. But, because of the style of writing, most scholars believe that another person wrote the maxims several centuries later.*

If you are a man among those who sit
at a place on your superior's table,
take what he gives, when it is placed under your nose.
You should look at what is in front of you—
do not pierce him with many looks!
Imposing on him is a horror to the spirit.
Do not speak to him until he calls!
One cannot know what seems evil to the heart.
You should speak only when he addresses you.
Then what you say will seem perfect to the heart.
A great man, when he is **at food**,
behaves as his spirit commands.
He will give to the man he favors. . . .

at food, eating

If you are an excellent man,
who sits in the **council** of his lord,
concentrate on excellence!
You should be quiet! This is better than a **potent herb**.
You should speak when you know that you understand:
only the skilled artist speaks in the council.
Speaking is harder than any craft:
only the man who understands it puts it to work for him.
If you are powerful, promote respect for yourself,
by wisdom, by calmness of speech!
Give no instructions except according to circumstances!
The **provoker** always begins to go wrong.

council, a group of people who advise

potent herb, powerful medicine

provoker, person who starts something

Do not be **haughty,** lest your heart be humiliated!
Do not be silent—but beware lest you offend
when you answer a speech with **ardor!**
Turn away your face! Govern yourself! . . .
Even the pleasant man, when he offends, has his way blocked.

< **haughty,** overly proud

< **ardor,** passion

Ancient Egypt: See Through History, by Judith Crosher (Viking, 1993), describes what life was like for many Egyptians, including rich people like Ptah-hotep.

18. Home at Last

THE TALE OF SINUHE, ABOUT 1960 BCE

This tale of adventure was first written down nearly 4,000 years ago, in Egypt's Middle Kingdom period. Children and adults read it, and it remained popular for almost a thousand years. The story begins with the death of the first pharaoh of Dynasty 12, Amenemhet I. Sinuhe, a member of the Egyptian royal court, hears the report of the king's death and flees, believing that there will be turmoil and trouble in the land. He spends many years in the area of the Levant (modern-day Syria, Lebanon, Israel, and the Palestinian territories). As he grows wealthy but also older, he feels the need to return home to Egypt and beg the new king's forgiveness, so that he can die and be buried in his homeland. When Sinuhe arrives in Egypt, he is not at all sure how he will be treated. Will the king, who is seen as a living god, punish him for leaving or welcome him home?

See chapter 8 in *The Ancient Egyptian World*

When dawn came and it was morning, I was summoned. Ten men came and ten men went to **usher** me to the palace. I touched my forehead to the ground between the sphinxes. . . . I found His Majesty upon the Great Throne set in a **recess** paneled with fine gold. As I **stretched out on my belly**, I lost consciousness in his presence. This God addressed me in a friendly way. . . . My soul fled and my body shook. My heart was not in my body: I could not tell life from death.

< **usher,** take

< **recess,** nook

< **stretched out on my belly,** lay face-down as a sign of respect

His Majesty said to one of these Companions: "Lift him up and let him speak to me." And His Majesty said: "See you have returned,

ravaged, damaged>

timorous, fearful>

now that you have roamed the foreign lands. Exile has **ravaged** you; you have grown old. Old age has caught up with you. The burial of your body is no small matter. . . . " I feared punishment and I answered with a **timorous** answer: "What has my lord said to me? . . . Fear is in my body. . . . I am in your presence. Life belongs to you. May Your Majesty do as he wishes."

Egyptians referred to people from the Levant as **Asiatics.**>

bedouin, nomadic> sheep herders who lived in tents

The royal children were then brought in, and His Majesty said to the queen: "Here is Sinuhe, who has returned as an **Asiatic** whom the **bedouin** have raised. She let out a cry, and the royal children all shouted together. . . . His Majesty said: "He shall not fear, he shall be a Companion among the nobles and he shall be placed in the midst of the courtiers. . . . "

depilated, removed hair, usually by plucking>

sand-dwellers, people> who lived in the desert

day of mooring, day of someone's death>

I was assigned to the house of a king's son. Fine things were in it, . . . Every domestic servant was about his prescribed task. Years were caused to pass from my body. I was **depilated,** and my hair was combed out. A load of sand was given to the desert, and clothes to the **sand-dwellers**. I was outfitted with fine linen and rubbed with the finest oil. I passed the night on a bed. . . . Meals were brought from the palace three and four times a day, in addition to what the royal children gave. There was not a moment of interruption. A pyramid of stone was built for me in the midst of the pyramids. . . . So I remained in the favor of the king until the **day of mooring** came.

The full tale of Sinuhe can be found in Richard B. Parkinson, *The Tale of Sinuhe and Other Ancient Egyptian Poems, 1940–1640* BC (Clarendon, 1997). George Hart's *Ancient Egypt* (Eyewitness Books, Knopf, 1990) includes chapters that relate to Sinuhe, such as "Preparing for the Tomb" and "The Royal Court."

19. I Didn't Do It

"THE NEGATIVE CONFESSION," BOOK OF THE DEAD, NO. 125, 16TH CENTURY BCE

See chapter 6 in *The Ancient Egyptian World*

The Book of the Dead was a group of magical spells designed as a "cheat sheet" for getting into the afterlife. During the New Kingdom period (about 1570–1070 BCE*), scribes wrote it out on pieces of papyrus, and the family placed it with the dead. The Egyptians* *thought the dead person would read the words and therefore know the right things to say on his or her journey to the afterlife. "The Negative Confession" was to be spoken at a crucial moment in that journey; saying these words might inspire the gods to overlook any misdeeds committed by the dead person either on purpose or by accident during his or her lifetime.*

I have not committed wrongdoing against anyone.

I have not mistreated cattle. . . .

I have not done evil.

I have not daily made labors in excess of what should be done for me.

My name has not reached the **bark of the Governor**.

< **bark of the Governor**, boat the sun god Re used to cross the sky

I have not **debased** a god.

< **debase**, treat something as less important than it really is

I have not deprived an orphan.

I have not done that which the gods **abominate.**

< **abominate**, hate

I have not **slandered** a servant to his superior.

< **slandered**, spread lies about

I have not caused pain.

I have not caused weeping.

I have not killed.

I have not commanded to kill.

I have not made suffering for anyone.

I have not diminished the offering loaves in the temples.

I have not damaged the offering cakes of the gods.

I have not stolen the cakes of the blessed dead. . . .

I have not added to nor have I subtracted from the **offering measure. . . .**

< **offering measure**, the standard used for measuring an offering to a god

I have not encroached upon fields. . . .

I have not tampered with the **plummet** of the scales.

< **plummet**, lead weight

I have not taken milk from the mouths of children.

I have not deprived the flocks of their **pasturage. . . .**

< **pasturage**, fields for grazing

I have not trapped fish in their marshes.

I have not diverted water in its season.

I have not erected a dam against flowing water.

I have not extinguished a fire at its critical moment.

meat offerings, > meat offered to the gods on certain days

I have not neglected the days concerning their **meat offerings.**

I have not driven away the cattle of the god's property. . . .

I am pure, I am pure, I am pure, I am pure!

The Book of the Dead can be found in several translations, such as *The Egyptian Book of the Dead,* translated by Raymond Faulkner (Chronicle, 2000), in which the hieroglyphs are printed next to the translations. Lila Perl's *Mummies, Tombs, and Treasures: Secrets of Ancient Egypt* (Houghton Mifflin, 1987) is a good guide to Egyptian beliefs and practices concerning death.

20. My Daughter, the King

PHARAOH (QUEEN) HATSHEPSUT, THE PUNT RELIEFS AND INSCRIPTIONS, ABOUT 1490 BCE

See chapter 11 in *The Ancient Egyptian World*

The expedition sent by Hatshepsut, a queen who ruled Egypt, to Punt is one of the most interesting and mysterious in the history of Egypt. The exact location of Punt is still debated, but it is almost certainly in Africa, and most likely in the area of modern-day Ethiopia or the coast of Somalia. Hatshepsut claimed that the god Amun-Re had commanded her to send this expedition and that hers was the first formal trade delegation to reach the "Myrrh terraces" of Punt (though Hatshepsut did not go there herself). The reliefs and inscriptions documenting this successful excursion, and showing the sights of the voyage and the goods brought back to Egypt, are carved onto the walls of Hatshepsut's temple at Deir el-Bahri, across the Nile River from the capital city of Thebes. Although Hatshepsut was a woman, she sometimes was referred to as "the king himself" to show that she was the equal of a king.

Makere, another name > for Hatshepsut

[Proclamation of] the king himself, the King of Upper and Lower Egypt, **Makere. . . .** A command was heard from the great throne, an oracle of the god himself, that the ways to Punt should be searched out, that the highways to the **Myrrh-terraces** should be penetrated: "I will lead the army on water and on land, to bring marvels from God's-Land for this god, for the fashioner of her beauty." It was done, according to all that the majesty of this revered god commanded, according to the desire of her majesty, in order that she might be given life, stability, and satisfaction, like Re, forever.

< **Myrrh-terraces** were terraces in Punt where myrrh trees grew. Myrrh trees produced valuable incense used in religious ceremonies.

Utterance of Amun-Re, lord of Thebes: "Welcome! my sweet daughter, my favorite, the King of Upper and Lower Egypt, Makere, who makes my beautiful monuments. . . . You are the king, taking possession of the Two Lands, . . . Hatshepsut. . . . You satisfy my heart at all times; I have given you all life and satisfaction from me, all stability from me, all health from me, all joy from me, I have given to you all lands and all countries, wherein your heart is glad. I have long intended them for you, and the **eons** shall behold them until those **myriads** of years of usefulness which I have thought to spend. I have given to you all Punt as far as the lands of the gods of God's-Land.

< **eons** and **myriads,** a very long time and countless numbers

"No one trod the Myrrh-terraces, which the people knew not; it was heard of from mouth to mouth by hearsay of the ancestors. The marvels brought thence under your fathers, the Kings of Lower Egypt, were brought from one to another, and since the time of the ancestors of the Kings of Upper Egypt, who were of old, as a return for many payments; none reaching them except your carriers.

"But I will cause your army to tread them, I have led them on water and on land, to explore the waters of inaccessible channels, and I have reached the Myrrh-terraces.

"It is a glorious region of God's-Land; it is indeed my place of delight. . . . They took myrrh as they wished, they loaded the vessels to their hearts' content, with fresh myrrh trees, every good gift of this country."

For a picture-book biography of Hatshepsut, see Catherine M. Andronik's *Hatshepsut, His Majesty, Herself* (Atheneum, 2001). Another good book on Hatshepsut is *Hatshepsut and Ancient Egypt,* by Miriam Greenblatt (Marshall Cavendish, 2000).

21. The Sun Is the One God

AKHENATEN, "HYMN TO THE SUN," ABOUT 1340 BCE

See chapter 15 in *The Ancient Egyptian World*

During Dynasty 18, about the year 1340 BCE, *Egypt underwent a religious revolution. Led by Amenhotep IV, the Egyptian pharaoh who changed his name to Akhenaten, the religion of Egypt began to look suspiciously like monotheism, the worship of just one god. Worship of the usual pantheon of gods and goddesses was forbidden, and only the worship of Aten, the sun disk, was permitted. Akhenaten presented himself as the son of Aten. However, rather than being a religious revolutionary, as many scholars used to think, Akhenaten may have been a very savvy ruler who saw a way to use religion to help himself remain in power.*

Let your holy Light shine from the height of heaven,
O living Aten,
source of all life!
From eastern horizon risen and streaming,
you have flooded the world with your beauty.
You are majestic, awesome, bedazzling, **exalted,**
overlord over all earth,
yet your rays, they touch lightly, **compass** the lands
to the limits of all your creation.
There in the Sun, you reach to the farthest of those
you would gather in for your Son,
whom you love;
Though you are far, your light is wide upon earth;
and you shine in the faces of all
who turn to follow your journeying. . . .

exalted, praised >

compass, cover >

You are the One God,
shining forth from your **possible incarnations**
as Aten, the Living Sun,
Revealed like a king in glory, risen in light,
now distant, now bending nearby.
You create the numberless things of this world
from yourself, who are One alone—
cities, towns, fields, the roadway, the River;

possible incarnations, > forms that the god could take

And each eye looks back and beholds you
to learn from the day's light perfection.
O God, you are in the Sun-disk of Day,
Over-Seer of all creation
—your legacy
passed on to all who shall ever be;
For you fashioned their sight, who perceive your universe,
that they praise with one voice
all your labors.

And you are in my heart;
there is no other who truly knows you
but for your son, Akhenaten.
May you make him wise with your **inmost counsels,**
wise with your power,
that earth may aspire to your **godhead,**
its creatures fine as the day you made them.
Once you rose into shining, they lived;
when you sink to rest, they shall die.
For it is you who are Time itself,
the span of the world;
life is by means of you.

< **inmost counsels,** most private advice

< **godhead,** divinity or godliness

Eyes are filled with beauty
until you go to your rest;
All work is laid aside
as you sink down the western horizon.

Then, Shine reborn! Rise splendidly!
my Lord, let life thrive for the King
Who has kept pace with your every footstep
since you first measured ground for the world.
Lift up the creatures of earth for your Son
who came forth from your Body of Fire!

Akhenaten is among the kings who are profiled in *The Pharaohs of Ancient Egypt,* by Elizabeth Payne (Random House, 1998). Before and after the time of Akhenaten, the Egyptians worshiped many gods and goddesses. You can learn about them in *Gods and Goddesses of Ancient Egypt,* by Leonard Everett Fisher (Holiday House, 1997).

22. A Phony Victory

RAMESSES II, QADESH BATTLE INSCRIPTIONS, 13TH CENTURY BCE

See chapter 18 in *The Ancient Egyptian World*

In 1274 BCE, the Egyptians and their enemies the Hittites from Hatti (now Turkey) met in a great battle at the city of Qadesh. The winner would control the region of the Levant. As near as historians can figure, the battle ended in a tie, but both the king of Egypt and the king of the Hittites claimed victory in their inscriptions! Ramesses II, king of Egypt, recorded his version of the tale in a number of places back home in Egypt. He wrote about his victory on the walls of temples at Abydos, Luxor, Karnak, Abu Simbel, and in the temple associated with his own tomb, the Ramesseum, located across the Nile River from Thebes.

chariotry, soldiers who fought in chariots >
Mont, a war god >
chaff, the outside of grain, or something useless >
extol, praise >
heed, listen to >

Now when my soldiers and **chariotry** saw
That I was like **Mont,** strong-armed,
That my father Amun was with me,
Making the foreign lands into **chaff** before me,
They started coming one by one,
To enter the camp at time of night.
They found all the foreign lands I had charged
Lying fallen in their blood;
All the good warriors of Hatti,
The sons and brothers of their chiefs.
For I had wrecked the plain of Qadesh,
It could not be trodden because of their mass.
Thereupon my soldiers came to praise me,
Their faces bright at the sight of my deeds;
My captains came to **extol** my strong arm,
My charioteers likewise exalted my name:
"Hail, O good warrior, firm of heart,
You have saved your soldiers, your chariotry,
You are Amun's son who acts with his arms,
You have felled Hatti by your valiant strength.
You are the perfect fighter, there's none like you,
A king who battles for his army on battle day;
You are great-hearted, first in the ranks,
You **heed** not all the lands combined.

You are greatly victorious before your army,
Before the whole land, it is no boast;
Protector of Egypt, **curber** of foreign lands,
You have broken the back of Hatti forever!"

< **curber**, person who controls or restrains others

Ramesses II's reign is discussed in *The Pharaohs of Ancient Egypt*, by Elizabeth Payne (Random House, 1998).

23. The Workmen's Complaints

LETTERS FROM DEIR EL-MEDINA, 13TH CENTURY BCE

Many of the people who lived in Deir el-Medina, a small village located across the Nile River from Thebes, earned their living by preparing the tombs of the kings and queens of Egypt in the nearby Valley of the Kings and the Valley of the Queens. There were about 400 people living There during Dynasty 19 in the 13th century BCE. *They left behind many papyrus documents and ostraca—broken pieces of pottery with writing on them—that help us to reconstruct what daily life was like back then. These four letters give a close look at some of the Deir el-Medina workmen's concerns.*

See chapter 19 in *The Ancient Egyptian World*

The mayor of the West of Ne (Thebes) Ramose communicates to the foremen of the crew, namely, to the foreman Nebnefer and to the foreman Kaha and the entire crew as well. To wit:

Now the city **prefect and vizier** Paser has written me saying, "Please have the wages delivered to the **necropolis** crew comprising vegetables, fish, firewood, pottery, small cattle, and milk. Don't let anything thereof remain outstanding. Don't make me treat any part of their wages as balance due. Be to it and pay heed!"

prefect and vizier, high official and civil < officer

< **necropolis**, ancient cemetery

The draftsman Prehotep communicates to his superior, the scribe... Kenhikhopeshef: In life, prosperity and health!

What's the meaning of this negative attitude that you are adopting toward me? I'm like a donkey to you. If there is work, bring the donkey! And if there is **fodder**, bring the ox! If there is beer, you never ask for me. Only if there is work to be done, will you ask for me.

< **fodder**, food

The scribe Nakhtsobek to the workman Amennakht:

...What's up? What have I done against you? Am I not your **old table companion?** Has the time come when you must turn your back? What shall I do? Please write me of the wrong that I've done against you through the policeman Bes. And if you refuse to write me either good or bad, this day is really bad! I won't request anything else of you. A person is delighted when he is together with his old table companion. While certain new things are good to have, an old companion is better.

old table companion, > old friend

[Author and recipient missing]

What's the meaning of your refusing to go to the policeman Nebmehy and buy for me those six beams which he has in his possession? Although I mentioned this to you ten days ago, you didn't go.... It is not proper, what you've done. Besides, I gave you an old pair of sandals with the further request to buy a beam for me with them, but you wouldn't buy it for me....

A further matter: As for the fish which you sent us...it was only thirteen fish that were delivered to us. Five of them had been removed. Demand them from the one whom you sent up with them.

You can learn more about daily life from other letters in Edward F. Wente's *Letters from Ancient Egypt* (Scholars Press, 1990), as well as from Rob Alcraft's book *Valley of the Kings* (Heinemann, 2000) and *Valley of the Kings*, by Stuart Tyson Smith and Nancy Stone Bernard (Oxford University Press, 2002). *Builders & Craftsmen*, by Jane Shuter (Heineman, 1998), also describes the lives of tomb builders like those at Deir el-Medina.

24. If the Pen Fits, Use It!

PAPYRUS LANSING, 12TH CENTURY BCE

See chapter 12 in *The Ancient Egyptian World*

The beginning of this papyrus states that it contains instruction in "letter writing," but in fact it is mostly concerned with how great it is to be a scribe and how bad it is to have any other occupation. The royal scribe Nebmare-nakht, who lived during Dynasty 20, sometime between 1185 and 1070 BCE, *wrote the papyrus. He hoped to convince a young scribe to stick to his studies in order to avoid the hard labor of other jobs.*

Advice to the unwilling pupil:

Young fellow, how conceited you are! You do not listen when I speak. Your heart is denser than a great **obelisk. . . .**

< **obelisk,** tall, square pillar with a pyramid-shaped top

So also a cow is bought this year, and it plows the following year. It learns to listen to the herdsman; it only lacks words. Horses brought from the field, they forget their mothers. Yoked they go up and down on all his majesty's errands. They become like those that bore them, that stand in the stable. They do their utmost for fear of a beating. But though I beat you with every kind of stick, you do not listen. If I knew another way of doing it, I would do it for you, that you might listen. You are a person fit for writing. . . . Your heart **discerns,** your fingers are skilled, your mouth is **apt** for reciting.

< **discerns,** understands

< **apt,** suited to

Writing is more enjoyable than enjoying a basket of . . . beans. . . . Happy is the heart of him who writes; he is young each day.

All occupations are bad except that of the scribe.

See for yourself with your own eye. The occupations lie before you.

The washerman's day is going up, going down. All his limbs are weak, from whitening his neighbors' clothes every day, from washing their linen.

The maker of pots is smeared with soil, like one whose relations have died. His hands, his feet are full of clay; he is like one who lives in the **bog.**

< **bog,** swamp

The cobbler mingles with vats. His odor is penetrating. His hands are red with **madder,** like one who is smeared with blood. He looks behind him for the **kite,** like one whose flesh is exposed.

< **madder,** plant used to make red dye

< **kite,** a bird of prey

The watchman prepares **garlands** and polishes vase-stands. He spends a night of toil just as one on whom the sun shines.

< **garlands,** wreaths

The merchants travel downstream and upstream. They are as busy as can be, carrying goods from one town to another. They supply him who has wants. But the tax collectors carry off the gold, that most precious of metals. . . . The carpenter who is in the shipyard carries the timber and stacks it. If he gives today the output of yesterday, woe to his limbs! The **shipwright** stands behind him to tell him evil things. . . .

< **shipwright,** someone who builds ships

The scribe, he alone, records the output of all of them. Take note of it!

Scribes were also responsible for many Egyptian advances in science and technology. *Science in Ancient Egypt,* by Geraldine Woods (Franklin Watts, 1998), describes the contributions of scribes.

25. Who Was the Thief?

REPORT OF WENAMUN, AROUND 1070 BCE

See chapter 22 in *The Ancient Egyptian World*

The Report of Wenamun is a story usually dated to the reign of Ramesses XI, about 1070 BCE. *The high priests of the temple at Karnak sent the priest Wenamun on a journey to fetch timber. Wenamun was to trade silver and gold for wood needed to build a ship for the sun god Amun. The story is about Wenamun's misadventures, including being robbed not long after he left Egypt and being shipwrecked on the island of Cyprus during his long journey back. When Egypt was at the height of its power, a man like Wenamun would have been treated with respect in the places he visited, but by this time, local princes in the Levant no longer bowed to the will of Egypt. This section of the story describes how rudely a Levantine prince treated Wenamun when the Egyptian priest discovered that one of Wenamun's own crewmen had stolen goods from his ship.*

riverine barge, boat used on a river >

rescripts, official announcements >

great Syrian sea, Mediterranean >

Tjeker, people of the Levant >

amphora, a large pot >

absconded, ran away >

deben, a weight measuring 93.3 grams >

Day on which Wenamun . . . departed to obtain lumber for the great and noble **riverine barge** of Amun-Re, King of the Gods. . . . On the day when I arrived at Tanis, at the place where Smendes [the governor of Tanis] and Tanetamon [Smendes's wife] are, I gave them the **rescripts** from Amun-Re, King of the Gods, and they had them read out in their presence. They said, "Will do, will do according to what Amun-Re, King of the Gods, our lord, has said." I stayed from the fourth month of the third season in Tanis. Smendes and Tanetamon sent me off with the ship captain Mengebet, and I went down to the **great Syrian sea** in the first month of the third season, day 1.

I reached Dor, a **Tjeker** town; and Beder, its prince, had fifty loaves, one **amphora** of wine, and one ox haunch brought to me. A man of my freighter **absconded,** stealing a golden vessel worth five **deben,** four silver jars worth twenty deben, and a purse containing eleven deben of silver. Total of what he stole: five deben of gold and thirty-one deben of silver.

I got up that morning, and I went to where the prince was and said to him, "I have been robbed in your harbor. Now not only are you the prince of this land, but you are also its investigator. Search for my money! Indeed, as for this money, it belongs to Amun-Re, King of the Gods, the lord of the lands. . . . "

And he said to me, "Are you serious, or are you joking? See here, I cannot understand this allegation you have made to me. If it were a thief belonging to my land who boarded your freighter and stole your money, I would repay it to you from my own storehouse until your thief, whatever his name, has been found. Actually, as for the thief who has robbed you, he belongs to you and he belongs to your freighter. Spend a few days here by me that I may search for him."

So I spent nine days moored in his harbor, and I went to him and said to him, "Look here, you haven't found my money. Please send me off with the ship captains and those who go to sea." But he said to me, "Quiet! If you wish to find your money, hear my words and do what I tell you."

The whole tale of Wenamun can be found in William Kelly Simpson's book *The Literature of Ancient Egypt: An Anthology of Stories, Instructions, Stelae, Autobiographies, and Poetry* (Yale University Press, 2003). The roles of high officials and priests, such as Wenamun, are described in *Pharaohs and Priests*, by Jane Shuter (Heinemann Library, 1998).

26. The King of Kush Conquers Egypt

KING PIYE, VICTORY STELA, ABOUT 735 BCE

The Kingdom of Kush was located along the Nile south of Egypt in what today is Sudan. For a thousand years, its people, called Nubians in later times, were under the rule of the Egyptians, who took gold, building stone, and wild animals from their land. But as Egypt grew weaker, the Kushites were able to strike back at the Egyptians. In this inscription, King Piye of Kush tells the story of his conquest of Memphis, an ancient capital of Egypt. Carved into a large slab of gray granite, this historical inscription shows how Kush managed to conquer Egypt around 735 BCE, several centuries after the end of the New Kingdom. Kushite control of Egypt lasted for about the next hundred years.

See chapter 22 in *The Ancient Egyptian World*

When day broke, at early morning, his majesty [Piye] reached Memphis. When he had landed on the north of it, he found that the water had approached to the walls, the ships mooring at the walls of Memphis. Then his majesty saw that it was strong, and that the wall was raised by a new **rampart,** and battlements manned with mighty men. . . .

rampart, protective barrier >

Then he sent forth his fleet and his army to assault the harbor of Memphis; they brought to him every ferry-boat, every cargo-boat, every transport, and the ships, as many as there were, which had moored in the harbor of Memphis, with the bow-rope fastened among its houses. There was not a citizen who wept, among all the soldiers of his majesty.

His majesty himself came to line up the ships, as many as there were. His majesty commanded his army saying: "Forward against it! Mount the walls! **Penetrate** the houses over the river. If one of you gets through upon the wall, let him not halt before it, so that the hostile troops may not **repulse** you. . . .

penetrate, enter >

repulse, force back >

Then Memphis was taken as by a flood of water, a multitude of people were slain therein, and others were brought as living captives to the place where his majesty was.

Now, afterward, when it dawned, and the second day came, his majesty sent people into it [Memphis], protecting the temples of the god. He . . . cleansed Memphis with **natron** and incense, installed the priests in their places. . . .

natron, a mineral used to dry out bodies for mummification and as a cleanser >

Then the ships were laden with silver, gold, copper, clothing, and everything of the **Northland,** every product of Syria, and all sweet woods of God's-Land. His majesty sailed up-stream, with glad heart; the shores on his either side were **jubilating.** West and east they were jubilating in the presence of his majesty; singing and jubilating as they said: "O mighty, mighty Ruler, Piye, O mighty Ruler; you come, having gained the dominion of the Northland. . . . Happy the heart of the mother who bore you, and the man who **begat** you. Those who are in the valley give to her praise, the cow that has borne a bull. You are unto eternity, your might endures, O Ruler, beloved of Thebes."

Northland, Lower Egypt >

jubilating, celebrating >

begat, fathered >

Two good books on Kush are *Egypt, Kush, Aksum: Northeast Africa,* by Kenny Mann (Silver Burdett, 1996), and *The Ancient African Kingdom of Kush,* by Pamela F. Service (Marshall Cavendish, 1998).

THE ANCIENT SOUTH ASIAN WORLD

Although writing in South Asia began in the cities of the Indus River valley before 3000 BCE, scholars have not yet been able to decipher the ancient script. There are only archaeological remains of the vibrant urban civilization that arose in South Asia around 2600 BCE, about a thousand years after cities appeared in Mesopotamia and Egypt.

The earliest works that we can read from the Indian subcontinent—poems, myths, and religious writings—come from the first millennium BCE, though some of the myths and stories were much older and passed down through oral storytelling. India gave birth to great religious traditions, including Hinduism and Buddhism, and most of its early writings are religious and contain important Indian ideas like reincarnation, or rebirth. Only later did fables, drama, and books on politics appear.

27. Hold Your Horses

UPANISHADS, ABOUT 700 BCE

See chapter 13 in *The Ancient South Asian World*

The poems called Upanishads are the spiritual heart of the scriptures of Brahminical Hinduism, a religion in which Brahma is the creator god. Upanishad *means "to sit down near someone"—wise men (or* rishis*) taught the Upanishads to students sitting down together outdoors. The lessons are very ancient. They were written down over a long period of time, in lines of poetry, in Sankrit, an ancient language from which the main languages of modern India and Pakistan, Hindi and Urdu, came. The earliest religion of ancient South Asia focused on ritual sacrifices, but the Upanishads instead concentrated on moral teaching.*

These writings were the first to express the idea of reincarnation—that a person might be reborn again and again as a human, an animal, or an evil spirit. How a person lives his or her life can affect what form he or she will take in his next life. Living a good life means a person will be reborn at a higher level of purity, whereas not following the rules can cause a person to be reborn as a lower creature. The real self is the soul—living in a physical body is only temporary. As a result, a person's goal should be to reach a level of virtue that will end the cycle of rebirth and allow the soul to be united with the Supreme Being, or Brahma, sometimes represented as the god Vishnu.

In the Upanishads, the charioteer is an image of a man in control of his senses (the horses). As a result, he can approach heaven.

Think of the soul as riding in a chariot,
With the body as the chariot.
The mind as the chariot-driver,
And the mind as the reins.

The senses, they say, are the horses;
The objects of sense, what they **range** over.
The self combined with senses and mind
Wise men call "the enjoyer."

range, roam >

Whoever has no understanding,
Whose mind is not constantly held firm—
His senses are uncontrolled,
Like the vicious horses of a chariot-driver.

He, however, who has understanding,
Whose mind is constantly held firm—
His senses are under control,
Like the good horses of a chariot-driver.

He, however, who has not understanding,
Who is unmindful and ever impure,
Reaches not the goal,
But goes on to reincarnation.

He, however, who has understanding,
Who is mindful and ever pure,
Reaches the goal
From which he is born no more.

He, however, who has the understanding of a chariot-driver,
A man who reins in his mind—
He reaches the end of his journey,
That highest place of Vishnu.

Madhu Bazaz Wangu's *Hinduism* (Facts on File, 2001) offers a good basic guide to the Hindu religion. Linda Johnsen, an American Hindu, explains her religion in *A Complete Idiot's Guide to Hinduism* (Alpha Books, 2001). A selection of the Upanishads is also available in *The Upanishads* (Penguin, 1965).

28. "Great Warrior, Carry on Your Fight"

THE BHAGAVAD GITA, FROM THE MAHABHARATA, ABOUT 500 BCE

See chapter 12 in *The Ancient South Asian World*

The greatest epic poem of ancient India, the Maharabharata, *describes a vast armed struggle between two noble families in about 1000* BCE. *The poem first took shape about 500* BCE, *although it continued to be expanded for centuries. The poem is 200,000 lines long—probably the longest poem ever written. The stories told in it remain important even today in South Asia.*

In a key moment near the climax of the Maharabharata, *the warrior Arjuna loses heart and does not wish to battle against his friends and relatives. Krishna, an incarnation, or human form, of the god Vishnu, is Arjuna's charioteer, and he reminds Arjuna of his duty to fight. Krishna's discussion with Arjuna is called the Bhagavad Gita. For thousands of years, Hindu followers of Vishnu and Krishna have put the Bhagavad Gita at the core of their belief. At one point in the story, the human Krishna reveals his terrifying identity as Vishnu—"I am Death, the All-Destroyer"—to show Arjuna that God includes everything in the universe, both love and death.*

In this passage Krishna explains the immortality of the soul, the process of reincarnation, and the soul's eventual union with God. He also says that bodies are of little value, because only the soul cannot be destroyed. If Arjuna wishes to reach God, he must do his duty, which, as a warrior, means fighting and killing.

When Arjuna the great warrior had thus unburdened his heart, he said "I will not fight, Krishna," and then fell silent. Krishna smiled and spoke to Arjuna—there between the two armies the voice of God spoke these words:

KRISHNA

Your tears are for those beyond tears; and are your words words of wisdom? The wise grieve not for those who live; and they grieve not for those who die—for life and death shall pass away.

Because we all have been for all time; I, and you, and those kings of men. And we shall be for all time, we all for ever and ever.

As the Spirit of our mortal body wanders on in childhood and youth and old age, the Spirit wanders on to a new body: of this the **sage** has no doubts.

sage, wise person >

From the world of the senses, Arjuna, comes heat and comes cold, and pleasure and pain. They come and they go: they are **transient.** Arise above them, strong soul. The man whom these cannot move, whose soul is one, beyond pleasure and pain, is worthy of life in **Eternity.**

transient, passing, not lasting >

eternity, everlasting life >

The unreal never is: the Real never is not. This truth indeed has been seen by those who can see the true. Interwoven in his creation, the Spirit is beyond destruction. No one can bring to an end the Spirit which is everlasting.

For beyond time he dwells in these bodies, though these bodies have an end in their time; but he remains immeasurable, **immortal.** Therefore, great warrior, carry on your fight.

< **immortal,** living forever

If any man thinks he slays, and if another thinks he is slain, neither knows the ways of truth. The Eternal in man cannot kill: the Eternal in man cannot die.

Madhu Bazaz Wangu's *Hinduism* (Facts on File, 2001) and Linda Johnsen's *A Complete Idiot's Guide to Hinduism* (Alpha Books, 2001) provide background for the Bhagavad Gita.

29. The Path to Enlightenment

“

BUDDHA'S SERMON AT BENARES, ABOUT 500 BCE

Siddhartha Gautama was the son of the king of a small state on the border between modern India and Nepal. At age 29, Siddhartha gave up his wealth and social position to take to the road as a wandering holy man. One night, while he was meditating, Siddhartha was able to understand his own past and future lives and decided to teach these truths to others. He preached to his followers the Middle Path between luxury and simplicity. His followers called him the Buddha—"the enlightened one." His teachings spread throughout East Asia, becoming the foundation for one of the world's great religions.

Buddha's followers wrote down many of his sermons right after his death. The Buddha gave his first sermon to disciples gathered at the city of Benares. Part of that sermon was a lesson about how to reach Nirvana, or enlightenment. He discusses suffering, and how to conquer it by overcoming the desires that cause it.

See chapter 14 in *The Ancient South Asian World*

This, monks, is the Middle Path, of which the **Tathagata** has gained enlightenment, which produces insight and knowledge, which brings tranquility, higher knowledge, enlightenment, and Nirvana.

< **Tathagata,** someone who has reached enlightenment

1. Now this, monks, is the noble truth of pain: birth is painful; old age is painful; sickness is painful; death is painful, sorrow, **lamentation,** dejection, and despair are painful. Contact with unpleasant things is painful, not getting what one wishes is painful. In short the five groups of grasping are painful.

lamentation, mourning >

2. Now this, monks, is the noble truth of the cause of pain: the craving, which tends to rebirth, combined with pleasure and lust, finding pleasure here and there; namely, the craving for passion, the craving for existence, the craving for nonexistence.

3. Now this, monks, is the noble truth of the **cessation** of pain, the cessation without a remainder of craving, the abandonment, **forsaking,** release, nonattachment.

cessation, stopping >

forsaking, giving up, or going without >

4. Now this, monks, is the noble truth of the way that leads to the cessation of pain: this is the noble Eightfold Way; namely, right views, right intention, right speech, right action, right livelihood, right effort, right mindfulness, right concentration.

Madhu Bazaz Wangu's *Buddhism* (Facts on File, 2002) gives an overview of Buddhism and its spread throughout Asia, with a discussion of its major schools of thought, its philosophy, and its moral teaching.

30. From Pauper to Prince

KATAHAKA JATAKA, 300 BCE

See chapter 20 in *The Ancient South Asian World*

The Jatakas are stories that tell about the forms that Buddha took in past lives. These bodhisattvas *had done good deeds and, as a result, were reborn at a higher level of purity until they reached enlightenment. Buddhists used these tales to teach values such as kindness, honesty, and self-sacrifice. Some of these stories were popular folk tales that the Buddhists adopted because of their moral value.*

In this story, a slave boy named Katahaka, who had been raised in the household of a rich banker in the city of Benares, uses what he learned in the banker's house to trick the daughter of a rich man into marrying him. When the banker later discovers the trick, he investigates and learns that the slave has been a good husband. He chooses not to tell anyone about the boy's lies, but he makes sure the boy will continue to be a good husband by letting him know that he could be unmasked. By letting the boy have a good future, the banker shows that he is a bodhisattva *on the path toward becoming the Buddha.*

Once on a time when **Brahmadatta** was reigning in Benares, the Bodhisattva was a rich Banker, and his wife bore him a son. And the selfsame day a female slave in his house gave birth to a boy, and the two children grew up together. And when the rich man's son was being taught to write, the young slave used to go with his young master's tablets and so learned at the same time to write himself. Next he learned two or three handicrafts, and grew up to be a fair-spoken and handsome young man, and his name was Katahaka. Being employed as a private secretary, he thought to himself, "I shall not always be kept at this work. The slightest fault and I shall be beaten, imprisoned, branded, and fed on slave's **fare.** On the border there lives a merchant, a friend of my master's. Why should I not go to him with a letter **purporting** to come from my master, and, passing myself off as my master's son, marry the merchant's daughter and live happily ever afterwards?"

< **Bruhmadatta,** king of Benares

< **fare,** food

< **purporting,** claiming

So he wrote a letter, saying, "The bearer of this is my son. It is **meet** that our houses should be united in marriage, and I would have you give your daughter to this my son and keep the young couple near you for the present. As soon as I can conveniently do so, I will come to you." This letter he sealed with his master's private seal, and came to the border merchant's with a well-filled purse, handsome dresses, and perfumes and the like. And with a bow he stood before the merchant. "Where do you come from?" said the merchant. "From Benares." "Who is your father?" "The Treasurer of Benares." "And what brings you here?" "This letter will tell you," said Katahaka, handing it to him. The merchant read the letter and exclaimed, "This gives me new life." "And in his joy he gave his daughter to Katahaka and set up the young couple, who lived in great style.

< **meet,** very proper

Along with Madhu Bazaz Wangu's *Buddhism* (Facts on File, 2002), numerous collections of Buddhist writings are available, including W. Max Muller's brief *Wisdom of the Buddha: The Unabridged Dhammapada* in the Dover Thrift edition.

31. A Chinese View of Ancient India

FAXIAN, A RECORD OF BUDDHIST KINGDOMS, 414 CE

See chapter 22 in *The Ancient South Asian World*

Faxian (also spelled Fa Hien) was a Buddhist monk from China who made a long journey to see the places where the Buddha lived and to find the sacred Buddhist texts. His trip lasted 15 years (399–414 CE) and took him through central Asia, Tibet, the Indus and Ganges Valleys, and Sri Lanka. He returned to China by way of Southeast Asia. Faxian brought many Buddhist writings in Sanskrit, the ancient Hindu language, back to China and devoted the rest of his long life—he died at age 88—to translating them into Chinese.

Though Faxian's memoir of his journey is primarily concerned with Buddhist shrines and communities of monks, he also provides an outsider's point of view on ancient Indian society. He is surprised by the Indians' gentler punishments for criminals—unlike the Chinese, they did not behead or physically hurt criminals. He also surprised by the Indians' vegetarianism, and the presence of outcasts called Chandalas, or untouchables.

magistrates, government officials

corporal, physical

All south from this is named the Middle Kingdom. In it the cold and heat are finely balanced, and there is neither frost nor snow. The people are numerous and happy; they have not to register their households, or attend to any **magistrates** and their rules; only those who cultivate the royal land have to pay some of their income from it. If they want to go, they go; if they want to stay on, they stay. The king governs without beheading or other **corporal** punishments. Criminals are simply fined, lightly or heavily, according to the circumstances. Even in the case of repeated attempts at wicked rebellion, they only have their right hands cut off. The king's body-guards and attendants all have salaries. Throughout the whole country the people do not kill any living creature, nor drink intoxicating liquor, nor eat onions or garlic. The only exception is that of the Chandalas, or outcasts. That is the name for those regarded as wicked men, and they live apart from others. When they enter the gate of a city or a market-place, they strike a piece of wood to make themselves known, so that men avoid them, and do not come into contact with them. In that country they do not keep pigs and fowls, and do not sell live cattle; in the markets there are no butchers' shops and no dealers in intoxicating drink.

Kathryn Hinds's *India's Gupta Dynasty* (Benchmark, 1996) and J. Auboyer's *Daily Life in Ancient India: From 200 BC to 700 AD* (Phoenix, 2000) describe Indian society at the time Faxian traveled there.

32. Never a Dull Moment for a Good King

KAUTILYA, THE ARTHASHASTRA, ABOUT 250 BCE

See chapter 16 in *The Ancient South Asian World*

Kautilya was minister to the Indian king Chandragupta, founder of the Mauryan Empire—the first great South Asian empire. He was one of the chief authors of the Arthashastra, *the most important ancient Indian text on the science of politics: how a king should wield political and economic power. Ancient sources describe Kautilya as a dishonest schemer who cared only about the well-being of the king. The king followed his advice and set up a wide network of spies against enemies at home and abroad. The* Arthashastra *is often very practical about issues such as how to run a state, tax citizens, control a royal army, and boost the economy.*

Because Chandragupta came to power in the aftermath of Alexander the Great's conquest of the Indus Valley, his main concern was to strengthen his kingdom against foreign invasions. For this reason the Arthashastra *devotes a lot of attention to foreign policy. It says the best way to weaken your enemies is to make alliances with the enemies of your enemies—a policy that leaders still follow today.*

If a king is energetic, his subjects will be equally energetic. If he is reckless, they will not only also be reckless, but also consume his works. Besides, a reckless king will easily fall into the hands of his enemies. Hence the king shall ever be **wakeful.**

< **wakeful,** aware

He shall divide both the day and the night into eight segments of 1.5 hours, called *nálikas*. . . . Of these divisions, during the first *nálika* of the day, he shall post watchmen and attend to the accounts of receipts and expenditure; during the second part, he shall look to the affairs of both citizens and country people; during the third, he shall not only bathe and dine, but also study; during the fourth, he shall not only receive revenue in gold, but also attend to the appointments of officials; during the fifth, he shall send letters to his ministers, and receive the secret information gathered by his spies; during the sixth, he may engage himself in his favorite amusements or in **self-deliberation;** during the seventh, he shall superintend elephants, horses, chariots, and infantry, and during the eighth part, he shall consider various plans of military operations with his commander-in-chief. At the close of the day, he shall observe the evening prayer. . . .

self-deliberation, > studying or thinking about oneself

He shall, therefore, personally attend to the business of gods, of heretics, of ***Brahmins* learned in the Vedas,** of cattle, of sacred places, of minors, the aged, the afflicted, and the helpless, and of women;—all this in order . . . or according to the urgency or pressure of those works. All urgent calls he shall hear at once, but never put off; for when postponed, they will prove too hard or impossible to accomplish. . . .

***Brahmins* learned in the Vedas,** > people of the highest class, priests, who know ancient religious hymns of India

In the happiness of his subjects lies his happiness; in their welfare his welfare; whatever pleases himself he shall not consider as good, but whatever pleases his subjects he shall consider as good.

The complete *Arthashastra* (Penguin, 1992) is almost 900 pages, but T. N. Ramaswamy gives a useful brief selection from the book in *Essentials of Indian Statecraft: Kautilya's Arthashastra for Contemporary Readers* (South Asia Press, 1994).

33. How to Get the Brahmin's Goat

PANCHA-TANTRA, 200 BCE

See chapter 23 in *The Ancient South Asian World*

The Pancha-tantra *are stories written in Sanskrit around 200 BCE, though many were first created much earlier. They were later translated into Persian, Arabic, Chinese, and even Greek and Hebrew. These stories, which often deal with animals, later became a part of folk-tales such as the* Arabian Nights *and, in Europe, Chaucer's* Canterbury Tales *and La Fontaine's* Fables, *and even the fairy tales collected by the brothers Grimm and Hans Christian Andersen. The* Pancha-tantra *became some of the most widely known stories in the world.*

This tale talks about some animals that are considered unclean and how Brahmins—the highest class of people, the priests—should not touch them, but other classes can. The idea of what is clean and what is polluted and the idea that some classes cannot touch certain animals affected all parts of ancient South Asian society. The story describes what people can and cannot touch.

A Brahmin named Friendly had been tending the sacred fire in the cold weather of February and decided that it was time to make a sacrifice of a goat. He went to a nearby village to ask for a goat to be used in the sacrifice...

After receiving a fat goat he put it on his shoulder and made his way back to his sacred fire. On the way three **rogues,** who were starving and cold, spied him and decided to try and get the goat for their dinner.

< **rogues,** mischievous people

"Come now! If we could eat that creature, we could laugh at this freezing weather. Let us fool him, get the goat, and ward off the cold."

The first man approached the Brahmin and said: "O pious Brahmin, why are you doing a thing so unconventional and so ridiculous? You are carrying an unclean animal, a dog, on your shoulder. Are you ignorant of the verse:

> The dog and the rooster,
> The hangman, the donkey,
> The camel, **defile** you:
> Don't touch them, but pass.

< **defile,** make unclean or impure

The Brahmin replied that it was a goat and not a dog, and kept walking.

The next man came up to him and said: "Alas, holy sir, alas! Even if this dead calf was a pet, still you should not put it on your shoulder. For the proverb says:

> Touch not unwisely man or beast
> That lifeless lie;
> Else, gifts of milk and **lunar fast**
> Must purify.

< **lunar fast,** religious fast during full moon

Again the Brahmin angrily replied that it was a goat and kept walking.

Finally the third man tried to fool him. "Sir, this is most improper. You are carrying a donkey on your shoulder. Yet the proverb tells you":

If you should touch a donkey—be it
In ignorance or not—
You need must wash your clothes and bathe,
To cleanse the sinful spot.

goblin, mischievous, dwarf-like creature

Finally the Brahmin was so confused that he decided that the goat was really a **goblin** that kept changing its form, and threw it down and made for home, terrified. Meanwhile the three rogues caught the goat and had a nice dinner.

A collection of these amusing stories can be found in Krishna Dharma, *Panchatantra: "Five Wise Lessons": A Vivid Retelling of India's Most Famous Collection of Fables* (Torchlight, 2004).

34. Laws to Live By

THE LAWS OF MANU, ABOUT 100 CE

See chapter 21 in *The Ancient South Asian World*

The Laws of Manu is a collection in Sanskrit of ancient sacred laws and customs of South Asia. The Brahmins believed the work was written by Manu, the mythical father of the human race. This early teacher of religion and law had become a god, but he agreed to pass on these divine laws to human scribes. Most modern scholars believe that the Laws of Manu that we have today were first written about 100 CE, although they probably contain older material.

The passages here deal with the rules of varna, *that is, caste or class; how students should behave; and how women should be treated. The main castes are Brahmins (priests), Kshatriya (warriors), Vaisya (workers), and Sudra (slaves). The rules concerning students show a society in which elders were respected and obeyed, while women were "honored" as long as they were controlled by others in their family.*

Laws about caste (varna)

But in order to protect this universe He [Brahma], the most **resplendent** one, assigned separate duties and occupations to those who sprang from his mouth, arms, thighs, and feet.

< **resplendent**, shining brilliantly, splendid

To Brahmins he assigned teaching and studying the **Veda,** sacrificing for their own benefit and for others, giving and accepting of alms.

< **Veda,** ancient religious hymns of India

The Kshatriya he commanded to protect the people, to bestow gifts, to offer sacrifices, to study the Veda, and to abstain from attaching himself to sensual pleasures;

The Vaisya to tend cattle, to bestow gifts, to offer sacrifices, to study the Veda, to trade, to lend money, and to cultivate land.

One occupation only the lord prescribed to the Sudra, to serve meekly even these other three castes.

Laws about schooling

At the beginning and at the end of (a lesson in the) Veda he must always clasp both the feet of his teacher, (and) he must study, joining his hands; that is called the Brahmangali (joining the palms for the sake of the Veda). . . .

But to him who is about to begin studying, the teacher always unwearied, must say: Ho, recite! He shall leave off (when the teacher says): Let a stoppage take place! . . .

Both when ordered by his teacher, and without a (special) command, (a student) shall always exert himself in studying (the Veda), and in doing what is **serviceable** to his teacher.

< **serviceable,** useful

In the presence of his teacher let him always eat less, wear a less valuable dress and ornaments (than the former), and let him rise earlier (from his bed), and go to rest later. . . .

Let him not pronounce the mere name of his teacher (without adding an **honorific** title) behind his back even, and let him not mimic his gait, speech, and **deportment.**

< **honorific,** respectful

< **deportment,** conduct

Laws about women

Women must be honored and **adorned** by their fathers, brothers, husbands, and brothers-in-law, who desire (their own) welfare.

< **adorned,** decorated

Where women are honored, there the gods are pleased; but where they are not honored, no sacred rite yields rewards.

Where the female relations live in grief, the family soon wholly **perishes;** but that family where they are not unhappy ever prospers.

perishes, dies or is ruined

Her father protects (her) in childhood, her husband protects (her) in youth, and her sons protect (her) in old age; a woman is never fit for independence.

Reprehensible is the father who gives not his daughter in marriage at the proper time; reprehensible is the husband who does not make his wife pregnant, and reprehensible is the son who does not protect his mother after her husband has died.

reprehensible, deserving blame

Wendy Doniger has a complete translation of *The Laws of Manu* in the Penguin Classics series (1991).

35. "Treat Me As a King Should"

ARRIAN, THE CAMPAIGNS OF ALEXANDER, 130 CE

See chapter 16 in *The Ancient South Asian World*

Arrian was a Greek historian who lived under the Roman Empire. He was trained as a philosopher and then served in Roman administration as the governor of a province. His books include The Anabasis of Alexander, *about the march across Asia to India undertaken by Alexander the Great, the Macedonian king, and the* Indika, *about the king's time in the Indus Valley and the return of his fleet.*

The king that the Greeks called Porus—Paurava, in Sanskrit—was the warlike ruler of the Punjab in northern India. After Alexander marched from modern Afghanistan through the Khyber Pass, he crossed the Indus River and camped beside a river across from Porus and his forces. Because Porus guarded the crossing with a herd of terrifying elephants, Alexander had to sneak his troops across the river by night at another crossing and circle around the enemy army. After being wounded nine times in battle, King Porus surrendered.

Porus was then brought to Alexander, who . . . rode and met him . . . with a few of the Companions. He reined in his horse and admired the size and handsomeness of Porus, who was over seven feet tall. He did not look like someone who had been defeated, but like a brave king who had fought honorably against another king.

Alexander spoke first and asked Porus how he wanted to be treated. Porus is said to have answered: "Treat me as a king should, Alexander."

Alexander, who was pleased with this answer, said: "I will do that for my own sake, Porus, but for your sake ask what you would like."

Porus replied that his request included all he wanted.

Alexander was even more delighted with that reply, so he gave back to Porus control over the Indians of his kingdom and even added territory to what he had ruled before. So Alexander royally treated that brave man, and afterwards found him to be loyal in every way.

Robin Lane Fox's *Alexander the Great* (Penguin, 1994) is a thorough biography of this amazing figure. Fox was the consultant on Oliver Stone's 2004 film about Alexander and even played a small role on screen. Robert Green has written a brief biography: *Alexander the Great* (Franklin Watts, 1996).

36. A Fishy Story

KALIDASA, SHAKUNTALA, 400 CE

See chapter 22 in *The Ancient South Asian World*

Shakuntala *is one of the most popular ancient Indian plays, written by the poet Kalidasa, who probably lived during the reign of Chandra Gupta II, about 400* CE. *Unfortunately, we know almost nothing for certain about his life.*

The story about the woman named Shakuntala comes from the Mahabharata epic. After her parents abandon Shakuntala as a child, a holy man finds her in the forest and raises her at his hermitage, a remote cottage. A king meets Shakuntala in the woods, falls in love, and marries her on the spot, but then leaves to return to his kingdom. She bears him a son, but when she brings the boy to the king, he says he doesn't know them. Fortunately, after divine intervention, the king recognizes the woman and her son.

In Kalidasa's version, the king gives her a ring with his name on it. When she forgets to give money to a beggar, the beggar puts a curse on her: her husband will not recognize her until he sees his ring. On her way to the capital, Shakuntala loses the ring and a fish swallows it. When the king does not know who she is and turns her away, she returns to the forest, devastated. In the meantime, a fisherman catches a carp and finds the ring in its stomach. He is arrested by palace guards and taken to the king. The passage below is the comic scene from the beginning of Act VI of Kalidasa's play, when the policemen harass the poor fisherman—until the tables are turned. Later, after the king sees the ring, he sends for Shakuntala and they are happily united.

The two policemen (*striking the man*). Now, pickpocket, tell us where you found this ring. It is the king's ring, with letters engraved on it, and it has a magnificent great gem.

Fisherman (*showing fright*). Be merciful, kind gentlemen. I am not guilty of such a crime.

pious, very religious >

First policeman. No, I suppose the king thought you were a **pious** Brahmin, and made you a present of it.

Fisherman. Listen, please. I am a fisherman, and I live on the Ganges, at the spot where **Indra** came down.

Indra, war god of Indo-Aryans >

Second policeman. You thief, we didn't ask for your address or your social position.

Suchaka, the second policeman's name >

Chief. Let him tell a straight story, **Suchaka.** Don't interrupt.

The two policemen. Yes, chief. Talk, man, talk.

Fisherman. I support my family with things you catch fish with—nets, you know, and hooks, and things.

Chief (laughing). You have a sweet trade.

Fisherman. Don't say that, master.

You can't give up a lowdown trade
That your ancestors began;
A butcher butchers things, and yet
He's the tenderest-hearted man.

Chief. Go on. Go on.

Fisherman. Well, one day I was cutting up a carp. In its belly I see this ring with the magnificent great gem. And then I was just trying to sell it here when you kind gentlemen grabbed me. That is the only way I got it. Now kill me, or find fault with me.

Januka, the first policeman's name >

perfume, smell >

Chief (smelling the ring). There is no doubt about it, **Januka.** It has been in a fish's belly. It has the real **perfume** of raw meat. Now we have to find out how he got it. We must go to the palace.

The two policemen (*to the fisherman*). Move on, you thief, move on. (*They walk about.*)

Chief. Suchaka, wait here at the big gate until I come out of the palace. And don't get careless.

The two policemen. Go in, chief. I hope the king will be nice to you.

Chief. Good-bye. (*Exit.*)

Suchaka. Januka, the chief is taking his time.

Januka. You can't just drop in on a king.

Suchaka. Januka, my fingers are itching (*indicating the fisherman*) to kill this robber.

Fisherman. Don't kill a man without any reason, master.

Januka (*looking ahead*). There is the chief, with a written order from the king. (*To the fisherman.*) Now you will see your family, or else you will feed the crows and **jackals.** (*Enter the chief.*)

< **jackals,** wild dog-like animals

Chief. Quick! Quick! (*He breaks off.*)

Fisherman. Oh, oh! I'm a dead man. (*He shows dejection.*)

Chief. Release him, you. Release the fishnet fellow. It is all right, his getting the ring. Our king told me so himself.

Suchaka. All right, chief. He is a dead man come back to life. (*He releases the fisherman.*)

Fisherman (*bowing low to the chief*). Master, I owe you my life. (*He falls at his feet.*)

Chief. Get up, get up! Here is a reward that the king was kind enough to give you. It is worth as much as the ring. Take it. (*He hands the fisherman a bracelet.*)

Fisherman (*joyfully taking it*). Much obliged.

Januka. He is much obliged to the king. Just as if he had been taken from the **stake** and put on an **elephant's back.**

< **stake,** a post used for executions; **elephant's back,** only important people rode on elephants

Suchaka. Chief, the reward shows that the king thought a lot of the ring. The gem must be worth something.

Chief. No, it wasn't the fine gem that pleased the king. It was this way.

The two policemen. Well?

Chief. I think, when the king saw it, he remembered somebody he loves. You know how dignified he is usually. But as soon as he saw it, he broke down for a moment.

Suchaka. You have done the king a good turn, chief.

Januka. All for the sake of this fish-killer, it seems to me. (*He looks enviously at the fisherman.*)

Fisherman. Take half of it, masters, to pay for something to eat and drink.

Januka. Fisherman, you are the biggest and best friend I've got.

Arthur Ryder's translation of this play has been reissued as *The Recognition of Sakuntala* (Dover, 2003).

THE ANCIENT CHINESE WORLD

The earliest known Chinese texts were written on animal shoulder bones and turtle shells. These might seem like odd writing materials, but the ancient Chinese probably wrote on silk and parchment as well. But, because they disintegrate quickly in the ground, these objects fell apart many centuries ago.

Unlike the scripts used by other ancient civilizations, the Chinese system gave a sign to each word, not to each vowel or consonant sound (as in the Greek, Latin, Hebrew, and Sanskrit alphabets) or to each syllable (as in Mesopotamian cuneiform and Egyptian hieroglyphs).

At some points in Chinese history, many books and documents were destroyed on purpose by kings who did not approve of what they said. So, just as in ancient Greece and Rome, the writings that survive for us to read are the ones that Chinese people really cared about, cared enough to copy them carefully by hand (a process that could take months). These include sayings by philosophers, stories, histories, instructions, and other documents deemed to be important.

You can read other important Chinese writers, such as Ban Zhao and Fang Xuanling, along with works credited to the philosopher Laozi, in the book *The Ancient Chinese World.*

37. Telling the Future with Oracle Bones

ORACLE BONES, 12TH AND 11TH CENTURIES BCE

See chapter 4 of *The Ancient Chinese World*

The ancient Chinese used oracle bones as a way to determine the future by asking questions of the gods. They posed a question, then heated and cracked an animal bone, then carved the question into it. Specialists "read" the pattern of cracks to figure out the answer to the question. Oracle bones were one of the first uses for writing in ancient China.

People posed the questions on these oracle bones about the harvest, revealing all the different forces that could affect whether they got enough food to carry them through the winter. The god of the Yellow River (Huang He), the second longest river in China, could harm the crops, or he could protect them against locusts. The king could plow a field himself as a ritual to make sure everyone's fields were fertile. Or he could make a sacrifice, of wine, for example. But you had to know the proper time of day for the sacrifice, and the oracle bones could tell you.

"Is it Di [the high god] who is harming our harvest?"
"Is it the Mountain who is harming the grain?"
"Is it the Yellow River who is harming the grain?"
"This season will the **locusts** reach to this city of Shang?"
"Should we announce the locusts to the Yellow River?"
"Should the king go to offer a wine sacrifice and perform the plowing ritual?"
"When we reach the fourth month, will Di order it to rain?"
"In praying for harvest, if the sacrifice is performed at sunset, will [the king] receive aid?"

locusts, swarming > grasshoppers that destroy crops

Oracle bones and other Chinese innovations are discussed in *Made in China: Ideas and Inventions from Ancient China*, by Suzanne Williams (Pacific View Press, 1996), and *Oracle Bones, Stars, and Wheelbarrows: Ancient Chinese Science and Technology*, by Frank Ross (Houghton Mifflin, 1989).

38. A Poem of the Seasons

BOOK OF POETRY, AROUND 600 BCE

Most of our information about ancient China comes from the richest and most powerful people in the country, and we know very little about how common people like farmers or tradesmen lived. But the following poem from the Book of Poetry, *China's earliest collection of poetry, describes the activities of the common people at different times of the year. Even farmers did a lot more than just farm. In the winter, they hunted for food and furs, and also collected blocks of ice to preserve food after the season changes. Rituals such as the presentations of offerings described in this poem were also important markers of the seasons, as people offered food to the ancestors and gods during particular months in hopes of fortune and long life.*

See chapter 5 of *The Ancient Chinese World*

In the fourth month, seeding is the yao grass;
in the fifth month, singing is the **cicada.**
In the eighth month you should harvest;
in the tenth month, the trees shed and leaves fall.
In the days of the first month, go and hunt badgers.
Catch those foxes and **raccoon-dogs**
and make fur garments for a young nobleman. . . .

In the days of the second month,
cut chunks of ice, *dong-dong!*
In the days of the third month,
store them in the ice house.
In the days of the fourth month,
rise early to present lamb and offer onions.
In the ninth month, things shrivel with the frost;
in the tenth month, clean the **threshing floor.**
Twin wine vessels are offered as a feast
and then slaughter lambs and sheep.
Enter that noble hall
and lift in a toast the **rhino cup:**
May you live forever and without end!

< **cicada,** a winged insect that makes a loud buzzing sound

< **raccoon-dog,** a type of dog, native to China, that looks very much like a raccoon

< **threshing floor,** floor of the room where grain is separated from the harvested plants

< **rhino cup,** cup made from a rhino horn

This poem, and others from the *Book of Poetry,* can be found in *The Columbia Anthology of Traditional Chinese Literature,* edited by Victor Mair (Columbia University Press, 1994). For more on agricultural practice in ancient China, see *Science in Ancient China,* by George F. Beshore (Franklin Watts, 1998). Julia Waterlow's *Ancient Chinese: Looking into the Past* (Thomson Learning, 1994) also includes a section about farming.

39. How to Stop Criticism

CONVERSATIONS OF THE STATES, FOURTH CENTURY BCE

See chapter 6 of *The Ancient Chinese World*

One of the most basic Chinese ideas about how to create a good government is that the ruler has to select reliable people as his officials and then listen to them in order to avoid mistakes. Kings, however, often do not like to listen to people less powerful than themselves. King Li, who lived in the ninth century BCE, was notorious as a bad ruler. He decides that rather than try to correct his own actions, he will stop people from criticizing him through harsh laws. But the power of popular opinion is like a natural force that no person can stop for long. The result of trying to stop a river from flowing is a flood. The result of trying to stop the people from speaking their minds is a rebellion.

Duke of Shao, an adviser to the king >

Wei was in the > northern part of China.

King Li was cruel, and the people of the state criticized the king. The **Duke of Shao** announced: "The people can't stand it." The king was angry, so he got a sorcerer from **Wei** and ordered him to search for his critics. Whenever he denounced someone, the person would be killed. None of the people of the state dared to talk, but they communicated with looks when they passed on the road. The king was delighted and he told the Duke of Shao, "I was able to stop the criticism. Now they don't dare talk." The Duke of Shao said, "You are just shutting them off. Damming the mouths of the people is more difficult than damming a river. When a river is blocked it breaks its banks and many are sure to be harmed. That is why when the Son of Heaven runs the government, he should have the dukes and ministers down to the various officials send in poems, the bards send in songs, the historians send in documents, the teachers send in warnings, . . . Only then can the king judge his own conduct on that basis. In this way the king can act and not go against the will of the people. . . ." The king would not listen and so none of the people of the state would dare to speak up. After three years, they exiled the king to Zhi.

Other myths and legends like this one are published in translation in a book by Cyril Birch and Rosamund Fowler called *Tales from China,* in the Oxford Myths and Legends series (Oxford University Press, 2000).

40. Which Is Worth More, Money or Loyalty?

LIU XIANG, STRATEGIES OF THE WARRING STATES, FIRST CENTURY BCE

The Warring States period, which lasted from 475 to 221 BCE, was a time of fighting between rival lords, when no king controlled all of China. A work of literature called Strategies of the Warring States, *which was probably compiled by the scholar Liu Xiang, tells us a lot about the society, ideas, and politics of the time. During this age, men with ideas traveled from state to state, looking for the chance to present their services and skills to a noble lord who would employ them and put their theories into practice. Men such as Lord Mengchang—who had a high position in Qi, one of the warring states located in modern Shangdong—gained a reputation for supporting scholars. Lord Mengchang came from the state of Xue, which was part of Qi, but lived at the king's court. Many of the brightest thinkers of the day lived under Lord Mengchang's roof as advisers, almost like part of the extended family. This story is about a poor man named Feng Xuan, who offered his services to Lord Mengchang. Although he did not claim to have any talents, he turned out to be the one person who could assure Lord Mengchang's safety.*

See chapter 7 of *The Ancient Chinese World*

There was a man from Qi named Feng Xuan, who was so poor he could not survive. He sent someone to ask Lord Mengchang if he could be part of his household. Lord Mengchang asked him, "What do you like to do?" He said, "Nothing." Lord Mengchang asked him, "What abilities do you have?" He replied, "None." Lord Mengchang accepted him with a laugh. . . .

Later, Lord Mengchang sent out a notice asking who was skilled in keeping accounts and could draw up documents and collect debts in Xue. Feng Xuan wrote saying, "I can."... As he was about to leave, he asked, "When I have collected all the debts, what shall I buy with the money?" Lord Mengchang said, "Buy whatever you think my household needs."

A **debt contract** was drawn up when someone borrowed money or goods. Half of the contract went to the borrower, half to the lender. When the borrower paid off his debt, he would bring his half with him and he was given the other half by the lender. >

Feng Xuan galloped off to Xue and had a clerk assemble all the people who owed money to come with their halves of the **debt contract.** When the two halves of the contracts had been brought together, he arose and, feigning Lord Mengchang's command, forgave all the debts. He burned the contracts and the people all shouted, "Long live [Lord Mengchang]!"

harem, a group of women in a household, often including several wives of the same man >

Feng Xuan rushed back to Qi and requested an audience with Lord Mengchang the next morning. Lord Mengchang, startled by his speed, received him in his formal robes, saying, "Did you collect all the debts? Why did you come back so quickly?" He replied, "I collected them all." "What did you buy with the funds?" Feng Xuan said, "You told me to buy what your household lacked. By my calculations, your palace is full of precious, rare objects, your stables are full of horses and dogs, and beautiful women fill your **harem.** The only thing your household lacks is the loyalty, so I bought you loyalty." Lord Mengchang said, "How do you buy loyalty?" He replied, "Now you own this little place Xue, yet you do not care about its people, but rather see them as a source of profit. So feigning your command, I forgave all the people's debts. When I burnt all the contracts, the people cried, 'Long live!' That is how I bought you loyalty." Lord Mengchang was displeased, and said, "Alright, go take a rest."

Lord Mengchang was an official of the King of Qi. When that king died and a new one took the throne, Lord Mengchang's services were no longer needed and he had to go home to Xue, where Feng Xuan had forgiven the people's debts.

A full year later, the [new] King of Qi said to Lord Mengchang, "I don't dare use the former king's officials as my officials." Lord Mengchang returned to his home state of Xue. When he was still fifty miles away, the people came out and welcomed him on the road, supporting the elderly and leading the young children by the hand. Lord Mengchang turned to Feng Xuan and said, "Today I see how you, sir, have purchased loyalty on my behalf."

The Warring States period is discussed in the illustrated Eyewitness Book *Ancient China* by Arthur Cotterell (Dorling Kindersley, 2000).

41. "The Virtuous Are Never Alone"

CONFUCIUS, ANALECTS, RECORDED SOME TIME BEFORE THE FIRST CENTURY CE

See chapter 10 of *The Ancient Chinese World*

Confucius, a great teacher and thinker, lived at the end of the sixth century BCE, *when many things were changing in China. With the land growing more warlike and unstable, Confucius tried to set new standards for a transformed world. He emphasized learning, but thought that thinking about matters was good, too, as long as you put your ideas into practice. He didn't think external things like clothes or fame were important. Instead, he encouraged everyone to follow the correct way. When his followers wrote down his sayings they put them in a particular order. Here are just a few of them, with many missing in between.*

When I was fifteen, I concentrated on learning; when I was thirty, I established myself; when I reached forty, I was no longer confused; when I was fifty, I knew the commands of Heaven; when I was sixty, my ears became obedient; when I reached seventy, I could follow the desires of my heart yet never go beyond the boundaries [of proper conduct].

If you study but do not reflect upon it, then your study will come to nothing. If you reflect on matters but do not study, you will be in danger.

Even if the barbarians had a ruler and the Chinese had none, they still would not be as worthy.

Wealth and a good reputation are what everybody wants, but if you cannot get them by sticking to your own Way, you should not keep them. Poverty and low status are what everyone

humaneness, kindness >

despises but if I get them by following my Way, I will not avoid them. If a gentleman avoids **humaneness,** how can he make a worthy name for himself? The gentleman does not abandon humaneness for an instant, even if he is in a hurry or in difficulties.

If there is a knight/scholar who is focused on the Way, but he is ashamed of ugly clothes and poor food, he is not worth talking to.

While your parents are alive, you should not travel to remote places, and if you do travel, you should have a definite destination.

The gentleman should be clumsy in speaking but careful in his actions.

The virtuous are never alone; they always have companions.

Russell Freedman's biography *Confucius: The Golden Rule* (Scholastic, 2002) includes a discussion of Confucius's teachings as well as what is known of the background to his life. The *Analects* are published in full, translated by Roger T. Ames and Henry Rosemount Jr., as *The Analects of Confucius: A Philosophical Translation* (Ballantine, 1998).

42. The Fox Borrows the Tiger's Majesty

LIU XIANG, STRATEGIES OF THE WARRING STATES AND GARDEN OF EXPLANATIONS, FIRST CENTURY BCE

See chapter 7 of *The Ancient Chinese World*

In some cultures, it is common for storytellers to use animals who think and act like humans; Aesop's Fables *is a good example. The following story is one of the few Chinese examples of this type of tale. In it, a fox, symbolizing a crafty man, makes use of the power of another (in this case, a tiger) for his own advantage. The story was told in the fourth century* BCE *to King Xuan of Chu, who asked whether a certain official was reliable. The king's adviser wants the king to understand that it is the might of the state of Chu that gives the official his authority and that King Xuan is the tiger who is being fooled by the fox. We don't know who originally composed this story, but we do know that it was written down in the third century and copied by the scholar Liu Xiang in the first century* BCE.

The tiger hunts the many animals and eats them. One day he caught a fox. The fox said, "You would not dare eat me. The Emperor of Heaven has made me ruler of all the animals. If you now eat me, you will be going against the command of the Emperor of Heaven. If you do not believe me, I will walk in front of you and you will follow after me, and you can see whether there is a single animal who does not run away when he sees me coming." The tiger thought this a good idea so they went walking, with the tiger in the rear. The animals all ran as soon as they saw them coming. The tiger did not realize that the animals were running away because they feared him, but instead thought they were in awe of the fox.

In another tale, a bright young lad uses an animal story to tell a very powerful man something he does not want to hear. The young man knows he cannot speak to the king, so he does something to draw attention to himself. When the king takes the bait and asks him why his clothes are wet, he has an excuse to tell a story that he hopes will convince the king. When talking to the King of Wu—a state in Suzhou, about 30 miles from modern Shanghai—this anonymous boy actually uses three different predators to let the king know that even though he thought of himself as the hunter, he was actually being hunted.

The King of Wu wanted to attack Chu and he announced to his advisers, "Anyone who dares to protest against this will die!" There was a small child in the household who wanted to protest but did not dare. So he went out into the rear gardens with a slingshot and pellets hidden in his shirt, and his clothes got covered with dew. He did this three mornings in a row. The king said, "Boy, come over here. What did you get your clothes all wet like this for?" The boy replied, "There is a tree in the garden with a cicada in it. The cicada lives high in the tree, chirping sadly and drinking dew, but he does not realize that there is a **praying mantis** behind him. The praying mantis is crouching low and is about to grab the cicada, but he does not realize that there is a sparrow at its side. The sparrow is stretching out its neck and is about to peck the praying mantis, but it does not realize the slingshot pellet is aimed at it from below. These three are all concentrating on the goody in front of them and not seeing

< **praying mantis,** a large, green insect

that trouble is behind them." The King of Wu said, "I see," and sent his troops back to their barracks.

Fables like this one are included in a collection put together by Tao Tao Liu Sanders called *Dragons, Gods & Spirits from Chinese Mythology* (NTC, 1994).

43. The Emperor's New Tomb

SIMA QIAN, RECORDS OF THE HISTORIAN, FIRST CENTURY BCE

See chapter 13 of *The Ancient Chinese World*

Sima Qian is often considered to be the father of Chinese history. He wrote an account not only of his own times, during the Han dynasty (202 BCE–220 CE), but also of earlier events, including the reign of the First Emperor of Qin, Qin Shi Huangdi, from 246 to 210 BCE. The tomb that Sima Qian describes here is in Xi'an, in western China, but archaeologists have not excavated it yet. They have uncovered an area around the tomb, where they found thousands of life-sized clay soldiers and horses, a whole army to protect the king after death. The tomb has probably been robbed since the time of the First Emperor, though archaeologists can always hope that the treasures that Sima Qian describes are still there, awaiting discovery.

In the ninth month he [the new emperor] buried the First Emperor at **Mount Li.**

When the First Emperor had just ascended the throne, he started to dig and construct the Mount Li Mausoleum. After he had united the world, more than 700,000 convict laborers from the world were sent there. They dug through three strata of springs, poured in liquid bronze, and secured the **sarcophagus.** Terra-cotta houses, officials, unusual and valuable things were moved in to fill it. He ordered artisans to make **crossbows** triggered by mechanisms. Anyone passing before them would be shot immediately. They used mercury to create rivers, the Jiang [or Yangtze], the Huang Ho [or Yellow], and the great seas, wherein the mercury was circulated mechanically. On the ceiling were **celestial bodies** and on the ground geographical features. The candles were made of oil of **dugong,** which was not supposed to burn out for a long time.

Mount Li, in the modern area of Xian, a manmade mound that looks like a hill >

sarcophagus, a stone coffin >

crossbows, powerful bows for firing arrows >

celestial bodies, planets and stars >

dugong, water mamal, also called a sea cow >

. . . After the coffin had been lowered into the tomb, someone mentioned that the artisans who made the mechanisms knew everything about the hidden treasure. The location of the hidden treasure and the important things could be disclosed by them. When the grand event was over and the treasures were put into place, the middle section of the tomb passage was closed up, and the door to the outer section of the passage was lowered, thus the artisans were all closed in the tomb, no one escaping. Trees were planted to make the tomb resemble a mountain.

Marcie Taylor-Thoma's article in the January/February 2002 issue of *Dig*, "Legend or Rumor?" features the archaeological work on the tomb of the first emperor. Another good source, with color photographs, is *The Emperor's Silent Army*, by Jane O'Connor (Viking, 2002).

44. Learning the Classics by Memory

“ WANG JIA, RECORD OF FORGOTTEN EVENTS, FOURTH CENTURY CE

For much of its history, China was a country where it was supposedly possible for a poor child to grow up to be rich, famous, and powerful by studying hard. But in fact, it was difficult for a poor child to become educated, because books were expensive and teachers required money for their instruction. Wang Jia was a magician and hermit who lived on a mountain with hundreds of followers. In the late fourth century CE *he wrote the* Record of Forgotten Events, *a collection of historical legends. In one legend, a young boy, Jia Kui, was so intelligent that he could remember difficult books just from hearing them read aloud. In reality, only someone of exceptional intelligence like this, or someone with a lot of luck, could go from a really poor family to an official career. Still, stories like this inspired many children to work hard at studying.*

See chapter 17 of *The Ancient Chinese World*

When Jia Kui was five years old he was brighter and kinder than the other children. His elder sister had been the wife of Han Yao, but having not produced a son, she had returned home to live. She was also famous for her chastity and intelligence. When she heard that someone in the neighborhood was reading books, whether morning or night, she would always bring Jia Kui so that he could hear the lesson through the fence. Kui would listen quietly without speaking and his sister was pleased by this.

The **six classic** books were as follows: *Yi Jing (Book of Changes)*, the classic of philosophy; *Shi Jing (Book of Odes)*, the classic of poetry; *I Li (Ceremonial Etiquette)*, the classic of propriety; *Shu Jing (Book of Documents)*, the classic of history; *Chun Qiu (Spring and Autumn Annals)*, a chronicle of Lu; *Yue Jing (Book of Music)*, a lost classic.

When he reached the age of 10, he could recite the **six classics** by memory. His sister asked Kui, "Our household is poor and we have never had a teacher set foot inside our door. How do you know about the classics and can recite them without missing a sentence?" Kui said, "I recall that you used to take me to listen to our neighbors read books. I remember every word." He then stripped the bark from the mulberry tree in their courtyard and made it into sheets, some of which he pasted to the doors and windows, and would recite and write down the texts. At the end of a year, he had the entire set of classics. People from his village, seeing this, would praise him, saying that he was without parallel in bringing the past to life.

swaddling, cloth used to tightly wrap babies

Students came to study with him from afar, some bringing their sons and grandsons wrapped in **swaddling.** They would camp near his gate and he would teach them the text of the classics orally. The donations of grain filled their storehouse. Someone said, "Jia Kui didn't use his own strength to plow [and make this food]; he just curled his tongue in reciting the classics. This is what they call 'plowing with your tongue.'"

City life and education are among the topics covered in Penelope Hughes-Stanton's book *See Inside an Ancient Chinese Town* (Warwick Press, 1986), which focuses on life in Loyang, the capital of the Han dynasty.

45. A Cunning Youth with Great Potential

“

CHEN SHOU, COMMENTARY ON BIOGRAPHY OF CAO CAO FROM SANGUOZHI, THIRD CENTURY CE

See chapter 20 of *The Ancient Chinese World*

Cao Cao, a Chinese general, was known for his brilliance in planning military strategy, but as a child he was one of the minor members of the very important Wang family. He was adventurous, which led some of his relatives to mistrust him. In the following account, Cao Cao plays a trick on his uncle so that his father won't listen to the uncle's stories of his bad behavior. This story comes from a commentary about a biography, or life story, of Cao Cao from a book known as Sanguozhi.

When young, Cao Cao was fond of **falconry** and racing dogs. He was **dissolute** and unrestrained. His uncle would often mention this to Song [his father], and Cao was worried about this. Later he ran into his uncle on the road. He put on a fallen face and a crooked mouth and when his uncle, thinking this strange, asked the reason, he said, "I have caught some evil disease." The uncle informed Song of this. Song was frightened and summoned Cao Cao, but his face and mouth were the same as always. Song asked, "Your uncle said you caught a disease, are you better already?" Cao replied, "I never caught a disease, I have just lost the love of my uncle, so he sees what is not there." Song's doubts were raised, and from that time, whatever the uncle told him about Cao Cao, he didn't believe him.

falconry, the sport of hunting with trained < hawks

< A **dissolute** person is someone who indulges in vices.

Childhood is the subject of Ken Teague's book *Growing Up in Ancient China* (Troll, 1993).

46. Courage Drives Off the Bandits

LIU YIQING, NEW ACCOUNT OF TALES OF THE WORLD, FIFTH CENTURY CE

Friendship is one of the Five Relations that followers of Confucius thought were basic to Chinese society, and poets often wrote about friends far away whom they missed. Liu Yiqing, a member of the royal family of the Song dynasty, collected stories about important writers and their sayings in his book the New Account of Tales of the World, *around 430* CE. *In this story, Xun Jubo, who is known only from this story, comes to the aid of a friend in need, and he will not abandon his friend even when threatened by violent warriors. The warriors are so impressed at his courage and selfless action that they abandon their attack and leave the area. Chinese history often provides examples of individuals who act nobly and inspire others to change their own conduct.*

See chapter 22 of *The Ancient Chinese World*

barbarians, foreign people believed to be inferior or uncivilized

marshaled, brought together in proper rank or order

Xun Jubo came a long way to look after a friend who was ill. Just then the **barbarians** were attacking the county seat and his friend said to Jubo, "I am about to die. You should go!" Jubo said, "I came from afar to see that you are alright. You order me to go, but forsaking my honor to save my own life, how could that be something this Xun Jubo would do?" When the bandits arrived, they said to Jubo, "When the great army arrived the entire county was empty. What kind of man are you, that you dare to stay here alone?" Jubo replied, "My friend is sick and I couldn't bear to leave him. I would like to offer my own life in place of my friend's." The bandits all said to each other, "We are a bunch of fellows lacking in honor and we have entered an honorable country." Then they **marshaled** their troops and returned home and the entire county escaped harm.

Ancient Chinese stories similar to this one have been collected by Linda Fang in *The Ch'i-Lin Purse: A Collection of Ancient Chinese Stories* (Farrar, Straus & Giroux, 1994).

THE ANCIENT GREEK WORLD

Ever since their arrival in Greece in the second millennium BCE, the people we call Greeks (they called themselves Hellenes) have continued to speak the same language. The earliest surviving works of Greek literature are two epics, the *Iliad* and the *Odyssey,* composed out loud by the blind poet Homer in the eighth century BCE. Later, Greeks wrote down Homer's poems and composed nearly every kind of literature: poetry, tragedy and comedy, history, philosophy, geography, biography, novels, speeches, and fables. In fact, the Greeks invented some of these forms. The Greeks wrote on papyrus—a kind of paper made from reeds that was invented in Egypt. Though only a small amount of ancient papyrus has survived, the great works of Greek literature were recopied again and again through the centuries and preserved in Greek monasteries. Though much has been lost—for example, fewer than 50 plays survive out of thousands that were produced—Greek literature had an enormous influence on Roman writers and on all later European literature.

In addition to passages from Homer, Aesop, and the Greek playwrights, the book *The Ancient Greek World* contains works from other Greek poets and the philosopher Socrates.

47. A Soldier's Family

HOMER, THE ILIAD, ABOUT 750 BCE

See chapter 5 in *The Ancient Greek World*

The Greek poet Homer has left us the first two masterpieces in European literature, the Iliad *and the* Odyssey*. These poems, called "epics" because of the grand scope of the story, were composed orally in the eighth century* BCE*. For centuries, they were sung at banquets for the entertainment of Greek nobles, and they were not written down until long after the poet's death.*

The Iliad *tells the story of a Greek expedition to the city of Troy on the coast of Asia Minor, in modern Turkey. Greek armies, led by kings Agamemnon and Achilles, besieged Troy for 10 years while the Trojans, led by Prince Hector, occasionally came out to battle the Greek heroes. In this episode, Hector returns from the fighting to see his wife and small son, who is frightened by his father's armor.*

Hector's wife, Andromache, knows that if Hector dies in battle, Troy will fall and she and her son will become Greek slaves. She tries to convince Hector not to fight, but he tells her that Fate alone will determine whether he lives or dies. They both must go about their business—he on the battlefield and she in the household—for they cannot avoid their destiny.

cringing, hiding in fear

horsehair crest, decoration on a soldier's helmet made of hair from a horse's mane

In the same breath, shining Hector reached down
For his son—but the boy recoiled,
cringing against his nurse's full breast,
screaming out at the sight of his own father,
terrified by the flashing bronze, the **horsehair crest,**
the great ridge of the helmet nodding, bristling terror—
so it struck his eyes. And his loving father laughed,
his mother laughed as well, and glorious Hector,
quickly lifting the helmet from his head,
set it down on the ground, fiery in the sunlight,
and raising his son he kissed him, tossed him in his arms,
lifting a prayer to Zeus and the other deathless gods:
"Zeus, all you immortals! Grant this boy, my son,
may be like me, first in glory among the Trojans,
strong and brave like me, and rule all Troy in power
and one day let them say, 'He is a better man than his
father!'—

when he comes home from battle bearing the bloody gear
of the mortal enemy he has killed in war—
a joy to his mother's heart."

So Hector prayed
and placed his son in the arms of his loving wife.
Andromache pressed the child to her scented breast,
smiling through her tears. Her husband noticed,
and filled with pity now, Hector stroked her gently,
trying to reassure her, repeating her name: "Andromache,
dear one, why so desperate? Why so much grief for me?
No man will hurl me down to Death, against my fate.
And fate? No one alive has ever escaped it,
neither brave man nor coward, I tell you—
it's born with us the day that we are born.
So please go home and tend to your own tasks,
the **distaff** and the loom, and keep the women
working hard as well. As for the fighting,
men will see to that, all who were born in Troy
but I most of all."

< **distaff,** stick used to hold fibers like wool when spinning thread

Hector **aflash in arms**
took up his horsehair-crested helmet once again.
And his loving wife went home, turning, glancing
back again and again and weeping live warm tears.

< **aflash in arms,** with weapons and armor flashing

Rosemary Sutcliffe's *Black Ships before Troy: The Story of the Iliad* (Delacorte, 1993) is a masterful retelling of Homer's great epic. Her descriptions bring Achilles, Helen, and even the gods to life. Ian Strachan, *The Iliad* (Houghton Mifflin, 1997), provides a lively abridgement of this noble, but bloody, story. Robert Fagles (Penguin, 1998) and Robert Fitzgerald (Farrar, Straus, and Giroux, 2004) offer translations of the complete poem.

48. Even Tough Guys Cry

HOMER, THE ODYSSEY, ABOUT 725 BCE

Odysseus had been away from his home in Ithaca for 20 years, 10 years fighting at Troy and another 10 years wandering on the seas. When he was shipwrecked and washed ashore, bedraggled and dirty,

See chapter 5 in *The Ancient Greek World*

he remained in disguise so he could confront the enemies who controlled his palace and threatened his wife, Penelope. When he first encountered his son Telemachus, whom he had left as a baby, he remained in disguise as a beggar. The goddess Athena always had a special love for Odysseus, and she transformed him into the hero he once was. When the hero allowed his son to recognize him, they both rejoiced at their reunion.

Athena stroked him with her golden wand.
First she made the cloak and shirt on his body
fresh and clean, then made him taller, supple, young,
his ruddy tan came back, the cut of his jawline firmed
and the dark beard clustered black around his chin.
Her work complete, she went her way once more
and Odysseus returned to the lodge. His own son
gazed at him, wonderstruck, terrified too, turning
his eyes away, suddenly—this must be some god—
and he let fly with a burst of exclamations:
"Friend, you're a new man—not what I saw before!
Your clothes, they've changed, even your skin has changed—
surely you are some god who rules the vaulting skies!
Oh be kind, and we will give you offerings,
gifts of **hammered gold** to warm your heart—
spare us, please, I beg you!"

hammered gold, > gold with a surface dented from being struck with a hammer

"No, I am not a god,"
the long-enduring, great Odysseus returned.
"Why confuse me with one who never dies?
No, I am your father—
the Odysseus you wept for all your days,
you bore a world of pain, the cruel abuse of men."

And with those words Odysseus kissed his son
and the tears streamed down his cheeks and wet the ground,
though before he'd always reined his emotions back.
But still not convinced that it was his father,
Telemachus broke out, wild with disbelief,
"No, you're not Odysseus! Not my father!

Just some spirit spellbinding me now-
to make me ache with sorrow all the more.
Impossible for a mortal to work such marvels,
not with his own devices, not unless some god
comes down in person, eager to make that mortal
young or old—just like that! Why, just now
you were old, and wrapped in rags, but *now,* look,
you seem like a god who rules the skies up there!"

"Telemachus," Odysseus, man of **exploits,** urged his son,
"it's wrong to marvel, carried away in wonder so
at sight of your father here before your eyes.
No other Odysseus will ever return to you.
That man and I are one, the man you see...
here after many hardships,
endless wanderings, after twenty years
I have come home to native ground at last.
My changing so? Athena's work, the **Fighter's Queen**—
she has that power, she makes me look as she likes,
now like a beggar, the next moment a young man,
decked out in handsome clothes about my body.
It's light work for the gods who rule the skies
to **exalt** a mortal man or bring him low."

At that Odysseus sat down again,
and Telemachus threw his arms
around his great father, sobbing uncontrollably
as the deep desire for tears welled up in both.

< **exploits,** heroic deeds

< **Fighter's Queen,** a nickname for Athena

< **decked out,** dressed

< **exalt,** raise high with praise; glorify

Rosemary Sutcliffe's *The Wanderings of Odysseus: The Story of the Odyssey* (Delacorte, 1996) is a lively retelling of the Greek epic. Peter Connolly's *The Ancient Greece of Odysseus* (Oxford University Press, 1999) tells the story of Odysseus' wanderings and discusses archaeological finds from Greece in the Bronze Age. Geraldine McCaughrean's *The Odyssey* (Puffin, 1997) also retells Odysseus' adventures. Robert Fagles (Viking, 1996) and Robert Fitzgerald (Farrar, Straus, and Giroux, 1998) offer translations of the complete poem.

49. Sly As a Fox

AESOP, FABLES, ABOUT 575 BCE

See chapter 9 in *The Ancient Greek World*

By the fifth century BCE*, the Greeks told fables that they believed had been written by a slave named Aesop. These fables were short stories, usually with animals as characters, intended to teach a moral lesson. Though we cannot be certain exactly when and where Aesop lived, his stories about speaking animals were very popular among both Greeks and Romans. There were several collections both in prose and poetry, containing a "moral" at the conclusion of each fable to teach a lesson. This fable is a simple lesson on the foolishness of saying bad things about someone.*

A very old lion lay ill in his cave. All of the animals came to pay their respects to their king except for the fox. The wolf, sensing an opportunity, accused the fox in front of the lion: "The fox has no respect for you or your rule. That's why he hasn't even come to visit you."

Just as the wolf was saying this, the fox arrived, and he overheard these words. Then the lion roared in rage at him, but the fox managed to say in his own defense: "And who, of all those who have gathered here, has **rendered** Your Majesty as much service as I have done? For I have traveled far and wide asking physicians for a remedy for your illness, and I have found one."

rendered, paid, given back

The lion demanded to know at once what cure he had found, and the fox said: "It is necessary for you to skin a wolf alive, and then take his skin and wrap it around you while it is still warm."

The wolf was ordered to be taken away immediately and skinned alive. As he was carried off, the fox turned to him with a smile and said: "You should have spoken well of me to His Majesty rather than ill."

MORAL: This fable shows that if you speak ill of someone, you yourself will fall into a trap.

Because most fables are less than one page, *Aesop's Fables,* translated by Olivia and Robert Temple in the 1998 Penguin edition is suitable for young readers.

50. What a Wonder Is Mankind!

SOPHOCLES, ANTIGONE, ABOUT 440 BCE

See chapter 20 in *The Ancient Greek World*

At religious festivals, the ancient Athenians attended performances of tragedies and comedies in outdoor theaters. In Greek tragedies, actors wore masks, and each played several different roles. There was also a chorus (playing characters) who sang and danced between the acts. The playwright often used the chorus to make general statements about life.

Of the Athenian tragic poets, Sophocles (496–406 BCE*) was most respected by the Greeks themselves. In his play* Antigone*, the chorus of old men sing of the resourcefulness of humans in conquering the sea and Mother Earth, taming all animals, and using language to build civilization. In fact, human beings have overcome every obstacle but death itself, and yet their intelligence leads them to disobey the gods and to sin.*

Wonders are many on earth, and the greatest of these
Is man, who rides the ocean and takes his way
Through the deep, through wind-swept valleys of **perilous** seas
That surge and sway.

< **perilous**, dangerous

He is master of ageless Earth, to his own will bending
The immortal **mother of gods** by the sweat of his brow,
As year **succeeds to** year, with toil unending
Of mule and plow.

< **mother of gods**, mother Earth

< **succeeds to**, follows

He is lord of all things living; birds of the air,
Beasts of the field, all creatures of sea and land
He takes, cunning to capture and ensnare
With **sleight of hand;**

< **sleight of hand**, a trick

Hunting the savage beast from the upland rocks,
Taming the **mountain monarch** in his lair,
Teaching the wild horse and the roaming ox
His **yoke** to bear.

< **mountain monarch**, mountain lion

< **yoke**, wooden bar between the necks of two animals such as oxen for pulling a plow

The use of language, the wind-swift motion of brain
He learnt; found out the laws of living together
In cities, building him shelter against the rain
And wintry weather.

subtlety, man's > shrewdness

There is nothing beyond his power. His **subtlety**
Takes every chance, overcomes every danger,
For every ill he has found its remedy,
Save only death.

O wondrous subtlety of man, that draws
To good or evil ways! Great honor is given
And power to him who upholds his country's laws
And the justice of heaven.

But he that, too rashly daring, walks in sin
In solitary pride to his life's end.
At door of mine shall never enter in
To call me friend.

Stewart Ross's *Greek Theatre* (Peter Bedrick, 1999) brings alive the production of Greek plays with a discussion of some of the Athenian playwrights. Peter Chrisp's *Greek Theater* (Raintree/Steck Vaughn, 2000) focuses more on the theater building, as well as equipment (such as masks) used in producing plays. A translation of *Antigone* is found in E. F. Watling's *Sophocles: Theban Plays* (Penguin, 1970).

51. A Greek Fish Story

HERODOTUS, THE HISTORIES, ABOUT 430 BCE

See chapter 8 in *The Ancient Greek World*

The Greeks frequently worried that the gods wanted people to have only a limited amount of good fortune. Therefore, they were afraid that if people were too lucky, the gods would send them some bad luck to make up for it.

The historian Herodotus (484–425 BCE) tells this story about an Egyptian king and his friend Polycrates, the ruler of the Greek island of Samos. Polycrates had made himself a tyrant by killing one rival and banishing another, even though they were both his brothers. Whenever he went off on a military campaign, he was very successful. Polycrates had what the Greeks called a guest-friendship with Amasis, the king of Egypt—a sort of understanding that each would entertain the other when he was in town and that they would also be allies in politics and warfare. When Amasis heard of Polycrates's increasing good fortune, he wrote to him:

"Please listen to me and take this response to your good luck: think what you consider most valuable—that which would be most painful to lose—and throw it away where no one can ever find it. . . ."

Polycrates thought this over, and because he understood that Amasis' advice was good, he asked himself what among his treasures would most break his heart if lost. He decided it was his ring, which he wore continually. It was bound in gold, and its stone was an emerald, the whole the work of Theodorus, son of Telecles the **Samian.** Polycrates decided to throw away this ring and did it in this way: he went aboard a ship himself, and ordered the boat to sea. When he was far from the island, he took off the ring in full sight of the onlookers and threw it into the sea. Having done so, he sailed back again, went to his house, and cried at what he had done.

< **Samian,** native of the island Samos in the Aegean Sea

Five or six days afterwards, the following thing happened. A fisherman caught a large and beautiful fish and thought it right that he should give it as a gift to Polycrates. . . . When the servants cut up the fish, they found in its belly Polycrates' **signet ring.** As soon as they saw it and took it out, they happily brought the ring to Polycrates, and told him how it had been found. The prince thought that this was a trick of the gods. So he wrote down in a letter all that he had done and what also had happened to him, and sent it off to Egypt.

< **signet ring,** ring with an engraved design to be used for sealing documents with wax

When Amasis read the letter from Polycrates, he realized that it was impossible for anyone to save his fellow man from his fate, and that Polycrates, despite his great success, would not come to a good end, since he had also found what he had cast away. Amasis sent a messenger to Samos and said he must dissolve the guest-friendship between himself and Polycrates. He did this so that, when some terrible disaster crushed Polycrates, Amasis might not feel in his heart the pain that he must for a guest-friend.

Since *The Histories* is a very long book, Samuel Shirley and James S. Romm have collected interesting passages with an introduction and notes in *On the War for Greek Freedom* (Hackett, 2003). Rex Warner (Penguin, 1954) provides a translation of *History of the Peloponnesain War.*

52. A Tribute to the Athenian War Dead

THUCYDIDES, HISTORY OF THE PELOPONNESIAN WAR, PERICLES'S SPEECH DELIVERED 430 BCE

See chapter 14 in *The Ancient Greek World*

The Greeks thought that the Athenian historian Thucydides, who lived in the fifth century BCE, *was the greatest of all historians because of his understanding of political and military events and his concern for accuracy. He wrote a history of the war between Athens and Sparta, which we call the Peloponnesian War. Thucydides explained the causes of war and its terrible effects. He also showed how the ambitions of politicians could affect the conduct of wars.*

Thucydides's great hero was the Athenian statesman and general Pericles. After the first year of the war, Pericles delivered a public funeral oration in honor of the Athenians who had fallen in battle. Abraham Lincoln used it as a model (in part) for his Gettysburg Address honoring the American Civil War dead. Pericles used the occasion to praise the government of Athens, and to show how Athenian democracy was better than other systems of government. It is a long speech, full of the pride of an Athenian who believed that his system was best. Yet despite the superiority of Athenian democracy, the Greeks lost the war in 404 BCE *and never again recovered their greatness.*

democracy, a government controlled by the people >

Our government does not copy our neighbors', but is a model to them. We are called a **democracy,** for the administration is in the hands of the many and not just a few. While there exists equal justice for everyone in private disputes, the claim of excellence is also recognized; and when a citizen is outstanding, he is preferred for election to public office, not as a matter of privilege, but as the reward of merit. Poverty is no obstacle, for a man may benefit his country even if his family is unknown.

The freedom in public life extends to our private lives, where we do not spy on each other, nor get angry with our neighbor for doing what he likes, nor even stare unpleasantly at him. While we are free in our private business, in public we are respectful of the authorities and for the laws. . . .

To sum up: I say that Athens is the School of Greece, and that the individual Athenian has the power of adapting himself to all kinds of challenges with style and charm. This is no empty boast, but the real truth—verified by the position to which these qualities have raised our country. For in its time of crisis, Athens alone among other cities is even better than her reputation. . . . And we shall not lack proof, since our mighty monuments will make us admired in our own time and in the future. We will not need the praise of Homer or any other poet whose verses seem unbelievable, for we have shown our courage on every land and every sea, and have everywhere left behind evidence of our good will and of our hatred. Such is the city for whose sake these men nobly fought and died; they could not bear the thought that she might be taken from them; and every one of us who survive should gladly toil on her behalf.

Peter Connolly and Andrew Solway's *Ancient Greece* (Oxford University Press, 2001) provides a good overview of ancient Greek civilization, including a discussion of Athenian democracy.

53. Is Writing a Good Thing . . . or Not?

PLATO, PHAEDRUS, 360 BCE

See chapter 23 in *The Ancient Greek World*

Many Greeks were unsure about whether writing was a good thing. Sometimes in a court case, people had more confidence in the testimony of a real live person than in a written document, because they figured a document could always be forged. In Phaedrus, *about a friend and student of Socrates, the philosopher Plato depicts his teacher Socrates telling the following story about the dangers of writing. He says that he has heard about an Egyptian god Theuth, who invented numbers and arithmetic and letters, trying to persuade Thamus, the king of Egypt, that all these things were valuable.*

Thamus makes the valid point that writing can weaken memory. Plato knew that in earlier times illiterate singers could memorize enormous poems, such as Homer's Iliad. *But now we use the library and the Internet, and memorizing texts is not necessary.*

Thamus said many things to Theuth in praise or blame of the various arts, which it would take too long to repeat; but when they came to the letters, "This invention, O king," said Theuth, "will make the

Egyptians wiser and will improve their memories; for it is a magic potion of memory and wisdom that I have discovered." But Thamus replied, "Most ingenious Theuth, one man has the ability to **beget** arts, but the ability to judge of their usefulness or harmfulness to their users belongs to another; and now you, who are the father of letters, have been led by your affection to think they have a power the opposite of that which they really possess. For this invention will produce forgetfulness in the minds of those who learn to use it, because they will not practice their memory. Their trust in writing, produced by external characters which are no part of themselves, will discourage the use of their own memory within them. You have invented an **elixir** not of memory, but of reminding; and you offer your pupils the appearance of wisdom, not true wisdom, for they will read many things without instruction and will therefore seem to know many things, when they are for the most part **ignorant** and hard to get along with, since they are not wise, but only appear wise."

beget, produce, create >

elixir, magic potion >

ignorant, lacking knowledge >

Though most young adults will find texts of ancient philosophy quite challenging, some may enjoy the stories of the trial and death of Socrates found in the inexpensive collection translated by W. H. D. Rouse, *Great Dialogues of Plato* (Signet, 1999).

54. Can a Philosopher Be So Wrong?

ARISTOTLE, POLITICS, ABOUT 330 BCE

See chapter 23 in *The Ancient Greek World*

The philosopher Aristotle was a student of Plato and the teacher of the Macedonian king Alexander the Great. Aristotle taught and wrote on an enormous range of subjects: politics, morality, literature, and many aspects of science, from biology to physics. His teacher Plato used reason to discover the ideals of government and justice. Aristotle's method was very different; he examined what he found in the world and then tried to describe it. In fact, as Alexander marched across Asia, he shipped back specimens of plants for his teacher to study. So before Aristotle wrote his book Politics, *he directed his students to prepare short reports on the constitutions of 168 Greek city-states. Aristotle thought that by collecting this information he thought he would be able to describe the best forms of government.*

Though he was brilliant, Aristotle was restricted by his method. If he observed that some men controlled other men, then he thought slavery was "natural." For the Greeks, slavery had nothing to do with racial difference, as it did later in North America; Greeks themselves could be slaves of other Greeks if they were captured in war or born to enslaved mothers. Similarly, Aristotle observed that since men held power over women, this too was what nature demanded. So in this passage Aristotle just describes what he sees as "natural," but he does not consider whether other forms of society might be better. For many centuries after Aristotle most Greeks and Romans continued to regard slavery as natural, though the Roman philosopher Seneca expressed his disapproval of the brutality of slavery. This was an important step toward the modern view that slavery— the ownership of one person by another—is against basic human rights and is thus unnatural.

We must consider whether it is good and just that anyone be a slave, or rather is not all slavery a violation of nature? There is no difficulty in answering this question, either in theory or in fact. For some people to rule and others to be ruled is not only necessary, but useful. From the hour of their birth, some people are marked out for domination while others are intended to be masters.... The same is true of animals in relation to men. Tame animals have a better nature than wild, and all tame animals are better off when they are ruled by man; for then they are safe. So the male is by nature superior, and the female inferior; one rules, and the other is ruled. This principle logically extends to all mankind....

Whereas the lower animals cannot even understand a principle, they obey their instincts. And indeed the use made of slaves and of tame animals is not very different; for both with their bodies **minister** to the needs of life. Nature would like to distinguish between the bodies of slaves and freemen, making the one strong for labor, and the other useless for physical work, but suitable for political life in both war and peace. But the opposite often happens—that some have the souls and others have the bodies of freemen. And doubtless if men differed from one another in the mere forms of their bodies as much as the statues of the gods do from men, all would acknowledge that the **inferior** class should be

< **minister,** care, give service

< **inferior,** lower

slaves of the superior. . . . It is clear, then, that some men are by nature free, and others slaves, and that for these latter slavery is both best and just.

 Margaret J. Anderson and Karen F. Stephenson's *Aristotle: Philosopher and Scientist,* (Enslow, 2004) is a clear discussion of the astonishing range of Aristotle's scientific and philosophical work.

55. Artists and Snobs

“ PLUTARCH, LIFE OF PERICLES, ABOUT 100 CE

See chapter 21 in *The Ancient Greek World*

The Greek author Plutarch wrote biographies of Greek and Roman statesmen to teach certain moral lessons. In his biography of the Athenian statesman Pericles, he puts forward the view that aristocrats should not become artists, but should appreciate art. A rich young man (and an occasional woman) was encouraged to study philosophy, but the Greeks saw poets, actors, and artists as little more than laborers. The low status of artists persisted many centuries after Greece and Rome, when artistic people were often thought to lead scandalous lives. Plutarch believed that an aristocrat should appreciate the art while keeping some distance from the artist.

Frequently we will see a product in which we take delight without having the slightest admiration for the person who made it. Perfumes and purple dyes, for example, are beautiful, but we do not consider perfumers or dyers to be anything other than vulgar, lower-class people not deserving of our respect. The philosopher Antisthenes was right when people told him that a certain Ismenias played the pipes beautifully and he responded, "Maybe so, but if he is, then he is a wretched human being; otherwise he couldn't be an excellent piper." Along the same lines, King Philip of Macedon, seeing his son Alexander playing music quite skillfully at a party, said "Aren't you ashamed, son, to play so well?" For a ruler honors the **Muses** sufficiently if, in his free time, he enjoys the performances of others. He does not need to play himself.

Muses, nine Greek > goddesses of the arts

low occupations, > humble jobs

Anyone who occupies himself in **low occupations** shows in the very pains he takes to do these useless things that he pays no attention to higher things. No honorable young man, seeing the statue of **Zeus** at Pisa, would ever want to be a sculptor like Phidias, or on seeing that of **Hera** at Argos want to be a **Polyclitus.** Nobody would want to become a poet just because of how much he enjoys the poetry of the poems of Anacreon or Philetas or Archilochus.

<**Zeus,** father of the Greeks gods; **Hera,** wife of Zeus: **Polyclitus,** sculptor

Rosalie and Charles Baker's *Ancient Greeks: Creating the Classical Tradition* (Oxford University Press, 1997) provides profiles of 37 important figures from ancient Greece, offering biographical details and a discussion of their importance in history.

56. Don't Mess with the Poet Telesilla

PAUSANIAS, DESCRIPTION OF GREECE, 150 CE

The Greek traveler Pausanias wrote down a great deal of information about monuments that have since disappeared and the stories that used to be told about them. Even though he lived long after many of the events he described, he had access to information that would be lost to us if he had not written about it.

Writing about the city of Argos, he tells the story of the poet Telesilla. She was a sickly child. When she sought advice from the gods about how to improve her health, she was told to devote herself to the Muses, the nine goddesses who were the patrons of artists. She did so, and became a well-known poet. Unfortunately, only a few words of this poetry survive, but according to Pausanias, she was well-known for something else as well.

See chapter 11 in *The Ancient Greek World*

Above the theater there is a temple of Aphrodite, and in front of the seated statue of the goddess is a slab engraved with a figure of Telesilla, the writer of the poems which lie as if they had been thrown down beside her feet. She herself is portrayed looking at a helmet which she is holding in her hand and is about to put upon her head. Telesilla was renowned among women for her poetry, but she was even more famous for the following achievement. Her fellow-citizens had sustained a truly indescribable disaster at the hands of the Spartans under Cleomenes son of Anaxandrides. Some had died in the battle itself. Of the others, who had taken **sanctuary** in the

sanctuary, place that offers safety or <protection

grove, some made the mistake of venturing out under a truce only to be slaughtered, and the rest, realizing the enemy's treachery, had stayed behind only to be burnt to death when the Spartans set fire to the grove. In this way Cleomenes led the Spartans towards Argos expecting a city of women. But Telesilla took all the slaves and all the male citizens whom youth or age had prevented from bearing arms and made them man the walls. And not only that: gathering together all the weapons that had been left behind in the houses or were hanging in the temples, she armed the younger women and stationed them at a place she knew the Spartans had to pass. The women stood their ground there, undismayed by the fearful war cry, and fought with so much determination that finally the Spartans decided they had better lay down their arms, since they realized that slaughtering an army of women wouldn't be much of a victory but being beaten by one would be shameful.

Fiona Macdonald's *Women in Ancient Greece* (Peter Bedrick, 1999) examines both the myths and realities of Greek women. She provides interesting information on women in the household, fashions, and occupations outside the home.

THE ANCIENT ROMAN WORLD

Even though the Romans founded their city in 753 BCE, literature in Latin did not appear until five centuries later. In fact, the first works written in Latin were plays and poems translated from Greek. Though Rome's literature was always in Greece's shadow, its poets, orators, novelists, philosophers, and historians have left us some very important writings. These books, once written on papyrus, were recopied in Christian monasteries throughout Europe and formed the core of education for more than a thousand years.

The Romans also carved texts in bronze and stone. The inscriptions of the emperor Augustus called the Achievements — quoted in the book *The Ancient Roman World*—survive only on stone. These hundreds of thousands of Roman inscriptions have great historical importance. And, if you like reading tombstones, you might find them fascinating!

The Ancient Roman World also contains passages from Plutarch's biographies about the Roman politician Cicero, the general Caesar, and the Egyptian queen Cleopatra.

57. Quiet in Back! Pay Attention, Please!

TERENCE, THE MOTHER-IN-LAW, 160 BCE

See chapter 18 of *The Ancient Roman World*

The earliest Roman plays were translated or adapted from Greek plays. The playwright Terence, who came as a slave from Africa to Rome in the second century BCE, *followed his Athenian models very closely. The plays often begin with a character called the prologue telling the audience about the plot and characters— there were no printed programs.*

In the third and second centuries BCE, *when plays were staged outdoors on temporary stages during religious festivals, the actors had to compete with street musicians, acrobats, trained animals, and even gladiators. In this excerpt from his play* The Mother-in-Law, *Terence uses his prologue to express in humorous terms the playwright's frustration with the distractions that caused the play to fail earlier.*

dogged, followed like a dog follows a scent

Now, please, listen politely to my request. I am again introducing Terence's play *The Mother-in-Law,* although I have never yet been able to find a quiet, attentive audience for it. Bad luck has **dogged** it. A favorable response from you, however, and your support of my efforts, will put an end to this bad luck. The first time I tried to present this play, my rivals for an audience were some famous boxers and then a tightrope walker as well. People gathered in noisy groups; there were shouts, and women's shrieks, and all this commotion forced us off the stage before the play was over. So, in order to give this new play another chance, I tried an old trick: I staged it a second time. And I was successful in holding the audience—at least to the end of the first act. But then a rumor spread that some gladiators were going to perform—and my audience flew off in a huge crowd, pushing, shouting, fighting to get a good spot at the gladiator performance. Well, I really couldn't keep my show going.

Today, however, there is no unruly mob. Everything is calm and quiet. I have been given a golden opportunity to stage this play, and you have been given the chance to pay honor to the dramatic arts. Don't allow, by your neglect, music and drama to fade away, appreciated by only a few. Let your support of the theater promote and encourage my own. As I have never greedily put a price value on my talent, as I have always maintained **adamantly** that my greatest concern was how best to serve your pleasure, so then now allow me this request. Terence, the playwright, has on good faith entrusted his work, indeed his very self, to my care and to your attention. Don't let wicked critics laugh wickedly at him, attacking him on all sides. Please, understand his situation and give us your undivided attention, so that other playwrights may be willing to write and so that I may be encouraged in the future to buy and produce new plays.

< **adamantly,** stubbornly or strongly

An edition of a Roman comedy prepared for young readers is Terence's *Phormio,* by William Alan Landes (Players Press, 2002). Other plays by the Roman comedy writers Terence and Plautus are included in *Four Roman Comedies: The Haunted House, Casina, or A Funny Thing Happened on the Way to the Wedding, The Eunuch, Brothers,* translated by J. Michael Walton (Methuen, 2003).

58. Home Sweet Home

HORACE, SATIRES, 30 BCE

Horace's father was a former slave who worked and saved to give the best Roman education to his son. Horace (65–8 BCE) became a friend of the poet Virgil, who introduced him to the emperor Augustus. With the emperor's gifts of money and a country estate, Horace was able to give up his job as a government clerk and devote himself entirely to poetry. He wrote four books of odes—short lyric poems about nature, love, and everyday life.

Horace's Satires *are conversational stories put in poetic form. In this poem, the poet takes a fable from the Greek writer Aesop to contrast the simple life of the countryside with the luxurious, but dangerous, life of the city. This story, made familiar by Horace and others who imitated him, has even inspired a television series about mice named Emily and Alexander. Aesop added a moral to the story: "It is better to live in self-sufficient poverty than to be tormented by the worries of wealth." Here a portion of Horace's poem is translated into English prose.*

See chapter 13 of *The Ancient Roman World*

Once upon a time, the Country Mouse, as the story goes, entertained the City Mouse in his poverty-stricken hole. The two mice were old friends. The Country Mouse was frugal and kept close watch on his supplies, but yet was able to relax his tight-fisted nature for the sake of hospitality. In other words, he didn't begrudge his friend carefully stored chick-peas or long-grained oats, and he carried to him a raisin and a half-eaten piece of bacon fat, since he wanted to tickle the **jaded** appetite of his guest with this varied dinner. But the City Mouse barely touched each morsel with **disdainful tooth,** while the master of the house lay stretched out on fresh straw and ate grain and weeds, leaving the choicer parts of the dinner for his guest. Finally the City Mouse said to the Country Mouse, "My dear friend, why do you want to live and suffer here on the ridge of a steep forest? Wouldn't you prefer the city and human dwellings to these rugged woods? Come on, take my advice and return to the city. Earthborn creatures have mortal souls; there is no escaping death, whether you are a large or small creature. So, my good fellow, live it up, while you may; enjoy life's pleasures. Live well, but always **mindful** that life is short."

jaded, bored as a result of too much experience >

disdainful tooth, > eating suspiciously

mindful, aware >

These words won over the Country Mouse and he lightheartedly skipped away from his home. The two mice traveled along the planned route, eager to creep under the city walls at night. And now night occupied the middle portion of the sky when both mice set foot in a luxurious mansion, where coverlets dyed scarlet gleamed on ivory couches, and many courses were left over from a large banquet on the previous evening, and the leftovers were ready at hand in heaping baskets. So the City Mouse settled the Country Mouse on a scarlet blanket, told him to stretch out, and then himself, as host, bustled about like a waiter, serving course after course, performing his waiter's duties perfectly, tasting everything which he served. The Country Mouse lay back and enjoyed his changed fortune, and played the role of the happy guest surrounded by luxuries. But suddenly a loud slamming of doors tumbled both mice from their couches. In panic they raced down a long hall, and were even more terror-stricken and confused when the lofty house resounded with the barking of vicious dogs.

Then the Country Mouse said, "I don't need this kind of life! Bye-bye! My forest and my little hole which is free from these dangers will console me as I eat my wild peas."

The complete poem may be found in *Satires of Horace and Persius*, translated by Niall Rudd (Penguin, 1982). A good collection of the fables of the Greek slave Aesop, whose animal stories reappear in many cultures, is Olivia and Robert Temple's *Aesop: The Complete Fables* (Penguin, 1998).

59. Be Sure to Look a Gift Horse in the Mouth

VIRGIL, AENEID, WRITTEN 19 BCE

See chapter 1 of *The Ancient Roman World*

The Roman poet Virgil's epic, the Aeneid, *recounts the legend of the Trojan prince Aeneas who fled from Troy to establish a new people—the Romans—in Italy. As he sailed across the Mediterranean, he landed in the North African city of Carthage, where he was welcomed by Queen Dido. At a banquet, Aeneas told the Carthaginians of the terrible story of the fall of Troy.*

After 10 years of war the Greeks were unable to capture Troy in war, so they tried a trick. They pretended to give up and sail away, leaving behind an enormous wooden horse, which they claimed was a gift to honor the gods. The horse was, in fact, full of armed Greeks hoping to be brought inside the city walls. The Trojan priest Laocoon warned his people of the trick, but the goddess Athena, who hated the Trojans, sent sea serpents to kill him and his sons. (The Trojan prince Paris had called Aphrodite, the goddess of love, "the most beautiful." She made the beautiful Helen fall in love with him, but the other goddesses were furious.) When the Trojans saw that the gods had punished Laocoon, they believed that the horse could safely be brought into the city.

And now there came upon this unhappy people another and yet greater sign, which caused them even greater fear. Their hearts were troubled and they could not see what the future held. Laocoon, the chosen priest of **Neptune,** was sacrificing a huge bull at the holy altar, when suddenly there came over the calm water from the island Tenedos (I shudder at the memory of it), two serpents leaning into the sea in great coils and making side by side for the shore. **Breasting** the waves, they held high their blood-stained **crests**, and the rest of their bodies ploughed the waves behind them, their backs winding, coil upon measureless coil, through the sounding foam of the sea.

< **Neptune**, Roman god of the sea

breasting, pushing the < chest against

< **crests**, ridges or tufts on top of their heads

Now they were on land. Their eyes were blazing and flecked with blood. They hissed as they licked their lips with quivering tongues. We grew pale at the sight and ran in all directions, but they made straight for Laocoon. First the two serpents seized his two young sons, twining round them both and feeding on their helpless limbs. Then, when Laocoon came to the rescue with his sword in his hand, they seized him and bound him in huge spirals, and soon their scaly backs were entwined twice round his body and twice round his throat, their heads and necks high above him as he struggled to pry open their coils, his **priestly ribbons** befouled by gore and black **venom,** and all the time he was raising horrible cries to heaven like the bellowing of a wounded bull shaking the **ineffectual** axe out of its neck as it flees from the altar. But the two snakes escaped, gliding away to the highest temples of the city—and making for the **citadel** of the heartless goddess Athena, where they sheltered under her feet and under the circle of her shield.

priestly ribbons, decorations on the priest's costume

venom, poison

ineffectual, useless

citadel, fortress

At the moment a new fear crept into all their trembling hearts. They said that Laocoon had been justly punished for his crime. He had **violated the sacred timbers** by hurling his sinful spear into the horse's back, and they all shouted together that it should be taken to a proper place and prayers offered up to the goddess. We broke through the walls and laid open the buildings of our city. They all buckled to the task, setting wheels to roll beneath the horse's feet and stretching ropes of **flax** to its neck. The engine of Fate mounted our walls, teeming with armed men. Unmarried girls and boys sang their hymns around it and rejoiced to have a hand on the rope. On it came, gliding smoothly, looking down on the heart of the city. O my native land! O Troy, home of the gods! O walls of the people of **Dardanus,** famous in war! Four times it stopped on the very threshold of the gate, and four times the armor clanged in its womb. But we paid no heed and pressed on blindly, madly, and stood the accursed monster on our sacred citadel. Even at this last moment **Cassandra** was still opening her lips to foretell the future, but God had willed that these were lips the Trojans would never believe. This was the last day of a doomed people and we spent it adorning the shrines of the gods all through the city with festive garlands.

violated the sacred timbers, because the horse was an offering to the gods, its wood was sacred

flax, plant fiber

Dardanus is an ancestor of Trojan kings.

Cassandra, Trojan princess who could tell the future, but was cursed so no one believed her predictions

Meanwhile the sky was turning and night was rushing up from the Ocean to envelop in its great shadow the earth, the sky and the treachery of the Greeks, while the Trojans were lying quiet in their homes, their weary bodies wrapped in sleep. The Greek fleet in full array was already taking the army from the island Tenedos through the friendly silence of the moon and making for the shore they knew so well, when the royal flagship raised high the fire signal and **Sinon,** preserved by the cruelty of the divine Fates, stealthily undid the pine bolts of the horse and freed the Greeks from its womb. The wooden horse was open, and the Greeks were pouring gratefully out of its hollow chambers into the fresh air, the commanders Thessandrus and Sthenelus and fierce **Ulixes** sliding down the rope they had lowered, and with them the soldiers Acamas, Thoas, Neoptolemus of the line of Peleus, Machaon, who came out first, Menelaus and Epeos himself, the maker of the horse that tricked the Trojans. They moved into a city buried in wine and sleep, slaying the guards and opening the gates to let in all their waiting comrades and join forces as they had planned.

< **Sinon**, a Greek secret agent

< **Ulixes** (called Odysseus in Greek) had the idea of the Trojan horse.

In addition to David West's translation (Penguin, 2003), Virgil's *Aeneid* is available in many other versions, including good translations by Robert Fitzgerald (Knopf, 1992) and Allen Mandelbaum (University of California Press, 1981). Penelope Lively's *In Search of a Homeland: The Story of the Aeneid* (Delacorte, 2001) provides a brief retelling of the *Aeneid.*

60. Listen to Daddy!

OVID, METAMORPHOSES, 8 CE

Ovid (43 BCE*–17* CE*) was an imaginative and sometimes outrageous poet whose poetry brought him both fame and grief. He often wrote about love: poems about the adventures of a poet in love; imaginary letters supposedly written by lovers of the past; and even a handbook for falling in love. Somehow he deeply offended the emperor Augustus and was sent into exile to spend his last nine years in Tomis, a remote town in what is now Romania.*

Ovid's epic Metamorphoses *is a poetic collection of mythological "transformations"—that is what* metamorphoses *means in Latin. So humans are changed into trees or flowers or animals or statues. Here*

See chapter 3 of *The Ancient Roman World*

is the story about the great craftsman Daedalus, who had built for King Minos a maze called the Labyrinth to imprison the Minotaur—a monstrous half-man and half-bull that could only be satisfied by eating humans—on the island of Crete. Minos would not allow Daedalus to leave the island, so Daedalus used his skill to make wings so that he and his son Icarus could fly home to Greece. But Icarus did not obey his father's instructions to take the middle way between sea and sun.

thward, prevent >

rustic, simple, of the country; **pan-pipe,** wind instrument with different length wooden pipes tied in a row; the musician blows across the tops of the pipes. >

hindered, slowed down >

Meanwhile Daedalus, hating Crete and his long exile, and filled with a desire to stand on his native soil, was imprisoned by the waves. "He may **thwart** our escape by land or sea," he said, "but the sky is surely open to us: we will go that way: King Minos rules everything but he does not rule the heavens." So saying he applied his thought to new invention and altered the natural order of things. He laid down lines of feathers, beginning with the smallest, following the shorter with longer ones, so that you might think they had grown like that, on a slant. In that way, long ago, the **rustic pan-pipes** were graduated, with lengthening reeds. Then he fastened them together with thread at the middle, and bees' wax at the base, and, when he had arranged them, he flexed each one into a gentle curve, so that they imitated real bird's wings. His son, Icarus, stood next to him, and, not realizing that he was handling things that would endanger him, grabbed laughingly the feathers that blew in the passing breeze, and softened the yellow bees' wax with his thumb, and, in his play, **hindered** his father's marvelous work.

When he had put the last touches to what he had begun, the craftsman balanced his own body between the two wings and hovered in the moving air. He instructed the boy as well, saying "Let me warn you, Icarus, to take the middle way, in case the moisture weighs down your wings, if you fly too low, or if you go too high, the sun scorches them. Travel between the extremes—take the course I show you!" At the same time as he laid down the rules of flight, he fitted the newly created wings on the boy's shoulders. While he worked and issued his warnings the aging man's cheeks were wet with tears; the father's hands trembled.

He gave a never to be repeated kiss to his son, and lifting upwards on his wings, flew ahead, anxious for his companion, like a bird, leading her **fledglings** out of a nest above, into the empty air. He urged the boy to follow, and showed him the dangerous art of flying, moving his own wings, and then looking back at his son. Some **angler** catching fish with a quivering rod, or a shepherd leaning on his staff, or a plowman resting on the handles of his plow, saw them, perhaps, and stood there amazed, believing them to be gods able to travel the sky. . . .

< **fledglings,** baby birds

< **angler,** fisherman

When the boy began to delight in his daring flight, and abandoning his guide, drawn by desire for the heavens, soared higher. His nearness to the devouring sun softened the fragrant wax that held the wings. The wax melted, and he flailed with bare arms, but losing his oar-like wings, could not ride the air. Even as his mouth was crying his father's name, it vanished into the dark blue Icarian Sea, named after him. The unhappy father, now no longer a father, shouted "Icarus, Icarus where are you? Which way should I be looking, to see you?" "Icarus" he called again. Then he caught sight of the feathers on the waves, and cursed his inventions. He laid the body to rest, in a tomb, and the island was named Icaria after his buried child.

Ovid's *Metamorphoses* is a huge collection of Greek and Roman mythology. Individual stories can be read in the translation by Horace Gregory (Signet Classics, 2001). Two books of Greek and Roman myths for young readers are Elizabeth Spires's *I Am Arachne* (Farrar, Straus, & Giroux, 1990) and Geraldine McCaughrean's *Roman Myths* (Margaret K. McElderry Books, 2001).

61. Slaves and Masters

SENECA, MORAL EPISTLE 47, 64 CE

See chapter 8 of *The Ancient Roman World*

The teacher and philosopher Seneca was born at Corduba in Spain in 4 BCE, but spent his entire career in Rome. Seneca became the tutor of young prince Nero, and remained his adviser when he first became emperor. Later, as Nero became more tyrannical and suspicious, he forced his old teacher to commit suicide.

As a thinker, Seneca followed the ideas of Stoicism, a school of philosophy that took its name from the colonnades (stoas) *in Greece where it was first taught. Stoicism's emphasis on duty and responsibility over personal desires was very appealing to the Romans. The Stoics also emphasized the brotherhood of mankind, so Seneca provides a not-very-Roman description of the relations between slaves and masters. Some scholars believe that early Christian thinkers read Seneca, and thus the Stoic attitude toward slavery affected Christian teachings.*

In this letter, Seneca argues for the common humanity shared by both masters and slaves, and points out that harsh masters make their slaves into enemies.

unpretentious, not showy, modest

Purse-proud etiquette means manners meant to show off a person's wealth.

repressed by the rod, punished with whipping

allusion, reference

I am glad to learn, through those who come from you, that you live on friendly terms with your slaves. This befits a sensible and well-educated man like yourself. "They are slaves," people declare. Nay, rather they are men. "Slaves!" No, comrades. "Slaves!" No, they are **unpretentious** friends. "Slaves!" No, they are our fellow-slaves, if one reflects that, Fortune has equal rights over slaves and free men alike.

That is why I smile at those who think it degrading for a man to dine with his slave. But why should they think it degrading? It is only because **purse-proud etiquette** surrounds a householder at his dinner with a mob of standing slaves. The master eats more than he can hold, and with monstrous greed loads his belly until it is stretched and at length stops doing the work of a belly; so that he is at greater pains to discharge all the food than he was to stuff it down. All this time the poor slaves may not move their lips, even to speak. The slightest murmur is **repressed by the rod;** even a chance sound—a cough, a sneeze, or a hiccup—is visited with the lash. There is a serious penalty for the slightest breach of silence. All night long they must stand about.

The result of it all is that these slaves, who may not talk in their master's presence, talk about their master. But the slaves of former days, who were permitted to converse not only in their master's presence, but actually with him, whose mouths were not stitched up tight, were ready to risk their lives for their master, to bring upon their own heads any danger that threatened him; they spoke at the feast, but kept silence during torture. Finally, the saying, in **allusion** to this same highhanded treatment, becomes current: "As many enemies as you have slaves." They are not enemies when we acquire them; we make them enemies.

Other philosophical letters of Seneca may be found in his *Letters from a Stoic* (Penguin, 1969), translated by Robin Campbell. Don Nardo's *Life of a Roman Slave* (Lucent, 1998) presents a picture of slavery in Rome.

62. Writing on the Walls

GRAFFITI FROM POMPEII, 79 CE

The walls of the Roman city of Pompeii were whitewashed each year and then covered with new graffiti—writing and pictures drawn or scratched on surfaces, often walls. One subject of the graffiti was election slogans. The meaning of some is clear, but others are hard to understand. Are the "thieves" really supporting Vatia, or did his enemies make them up as a "dirty trick"? The duovirs *are the two head officials of the city, while the* aedile *handled less important duties such as regulating the markets.*

See chapter 16 of *The Ancient Roman World*

The **muleteers** support Gaius Julius Polybius for duovir.

< **muleteers,** mule drivers

The petty thieves urge you to elect Vatia aedile.

Vote for Lucius Popidius Sabinus; his grandmother worked hard for his last election and is pleased with the results.

This advertisement promotes the coming gladiatorial games in the amphitheater of Pompeii. The mention of "awnings" means that large sails will be hung to provide shade to the spectators. The names are of Romans who owned the gladiators and made sure they were well trained.

Twenty pairs of gladiators presented by D. Lucretius Satrius Valens, priest of Nero Caesar for life, and ten pairs of gladiators presented by his son, D. Lucretius Valens, will fight in Pompeii on April 8, 9, 10, 11, 12. There will also be a suitable wild animal hunt. The awnings will be used. Aemilius Celer wrote this, all alone, in the moonlight.

At least some Pompeians were educated enough to recognize the first words of Virgil's epic poem, the Aeneid.

I sing of arms and the man (*arma virumque cano*)

Pompeians were particularly interested in love and money. Many graffiti writers express love, or anger at someone who rejected their love. Here the writer calls upon the goddess of love to curse his rival in love. Another Pompeian celebrates moneymaking.

> Lovers like bees draw out the sweet life.
> I beg you, Venus, let my rival perish.
>
> Hello Profit!
> Profit is joy!

Here someone has drawn an image of the Greek craftsman Daedalus's maze called Labyrinth in Crete. Perhaps a Pompeian child who was reading Ovid's poem about Daedalus in school drew this picture.

Labyrinth: Here the Minotaur Lives (*Labyrinthus: Hic Habitat Minotaurus*)

To learn about Pompeii, you might read Dale Brown's *Pompeii: The Vanished City* (Time-Life Books, 1992). It uses the findings of archaeologists to bring the ancient city to life. Another beautiful book is Peter Connolly's *Pompeii* (Oxford University Press, 1985).

63. The Prodigal Son

THE GOSPEL ACCORDING TO LUKE, NEW TESTAMENT

See chapter 24 of *The Ancient Roman World*

In the New Testament of the Bible, the word parable *usually means a story containing a moral lesson. One of Jesus's best-known parables is that of the prodigal son, which at first glance seems puzzling. One son takes his father's money and wastes it living wildly and doing things forbidden by Jewish law—including touching unclean animals such as pigs. Another son obeys the Jewish laws, remains at home, and is loyal to his father. When the father welcomes his wayward son home, the obedient brother is angry that his father ignores* his *loyalty and rewards his "bad brother."*

We might agree with the loyal son that the treatment is unfair, but that is exactly Jesus's point. The father's behavior is not about justice—his treatment of his sons is *unfair—but about a parent's unconditional love for his children. And that lesson applies to God's love for men and women. Like the parables of the lost sheep and the lost coin—which are also in the book called The Gospel According to Luke—the moral is that what has been lost becomes all the more precious. So, says Jesus, is the sinner who returns to God.*

Jesus continued: "There was a man who had two sons. The younger one said to his father, 'Father, give me my share of the **estate.**' So he divided his property between them.

< **estate,** family property, inheritance

"Not long after that, the younger son got together all he had, set off for a distant country and there **squandered** his wealth in wild living. After he had spent everything, there was a severe **famine** in that whole country, and he began to be in need. So he went and hired himself out to a citizen of that country, who sent him to his fields to feed pigs. He longed to fill his stomach with the pods that the pigs were eating, but no one gave him anything.

< **squandered,** wasted

< **famine,** shortage of food

"When he came to his senses, he said, 'How many of my father's hired men have food to spare, and here I am starving to death! I will set out and go back to my father and say to him: Father, I have sinned against heaven and against you. I am no longer worthy to be called your son; make me like one of your hired men.' So he got up and went to his father.

"But while he was still a long way off, his father saw him and was filled with compassion for him; he ran to his son, threw his arms around him and kissed him.

The son said to him, 'Father, I have sinned against heaven and against you. I am no longer worthy to be called your son.' But the father said to his servants, 'Quick! Bring the best robe and put it on him. Put a ring on his finger and sandals on his feet. Bring the fattened calf and kill it. Let's have a feast and celebrate. For this son of mine was dead and is alive again; he was lost and is found.' So they began to celebrate.

"Meanwhile, the older son was in the field. When he came near the house, he heard music and dancing. So he called one of the servants and asked him what was going on. 'Your brother has come,' he replied, 'and your father has killed the fattened calf because he has him back safe and sound.'

"The older brother became angry and refused to go in. So his father went out and pleaded with him. But he answered his father, 'Look! All these years I've been slaving for you and never disobeyed your orders. Yet you never gave me even a young goat so I could celebrate with my friends. But when this son of yours who has **squandered** your property. . . comes home, you kill the fattened calf for him!'

squandered, wasted >

"'My son,' the father said, 'you are always with me, and everything I have is yours. But we had to celebrate and be glad, because this brother of yours was dead and is alive again; he was lost and is found.'"

Other parables of Jesus are contained in The Gospel According to Luke in the New Testament. This book is included in all versions of the Christian Holy Bible.

64. A-hunting We Will Go

PLINY, LETTER TO TACITUS, ABOUT 105 CE

Pliny the Younger (61–112 CE), who was adopted by his uncle Pliny and took his name, was, like his uncle, a writer and Roman administrator. As a public speaker, lawyer, and member of the Roman senate, he reached the highest office, the consulship, in 98 CE and was a personal friend of the emperor Trajan.

In this letter Pliny tells his friend Tacitus, a historian and senator, about a hunting trip—fun for the rich while slaves do most of the work of tracking the animals. Pliny prefers to read books than to get outdoor exercise, so he expects his friend to laugh at him. He wants to assure Tacitus that he went hunting with a book in his hand. Sitting in the woods, he says, is a good place to think about literature, because Minerva, the patron goddess of literature, is in the woods just as much as the patron of hunting, Diana.

See chapter 18 of *The Ancient Roman World*

You will laugh, and well you may. I, that Pliny whom you know well, captured three wild boars, and very handsome ones at that! "You?" you will exclaim. Yes, me! Not that I interrupted my quiet and inactive studies, mind you. I just happened to be sitting by the nets. I didn't even have a spear or a lance beside me. Instead I had a stylus and some **waxed tablets.** I was busy composing thoughts and jotting down notes so that I would bring back tablets that were full even if my hands were empty. There is no reason for you to scorn this type of literary activity. In fact, it is amazing how the mind is stimulated by the movement and activity of the body. Moreover, the woods on all sides and the solitude and the very silence itself which hunting demands are also great **inducements** to creative thinking. And so, the next time you go hunting, take my advice and take along with you a picnic basket and a bottle of wine and your waxed tablets certainly. You will discover that Minerva roams the mountains as much as Diana.

< **waxed tablets,** wooden boards covered with wax used as a writing surface; a wooden stylus was used to scratch into the wax.

< **inducements,** things that persuade or influence

Peter Connolly and Hazel Dodge's *The Ancient City: Life in Classical Athens and Rome* (Oxford University Press, 2000) tells readers about how people lived in Athens and Rome. Eilis Dillon's *Living in Imperial Rome* (O'Brien Press, 1997) provides an introduction to everyday life in the city.

65. Roman Views of the Christians

PLINY, LETTER TO TRAJAN, 110 CE

See chapter 24 of *The Ancient Roman World*

About 110 CE the emperor Trajan sent Pliny the Younger to be governor of the province of Bithynia in Asia Minor—what is today Turkey. The Christian religion had grown rapidly in that area since the 50s CE. The apostle Paul had already written letters to Christian communities in Galatia and Ephesus in Asia Minor. Pliny often wrote to the emperor about the problems of government, and since Trajan was his good friend, the emperor himself responded instead of a palace official. But since the emperor had the entire empire to govern, his letters are briefer than Pliny's and more to the point.

In this letter to Trajan, Pliny is concerned about Christians, who are being accused by Romans of being disloyal to the emperor. There are even anonymous, or unsigned, pamphlets that denounce the Christians as atheists, or nonbelievers, since they refused to worship the Roman gods. After an investigation, Pliny dismisses charges against those who deny being Christians. The more difficult issue is what to do about those who confess that they are Christians, but say they have done nothing wrong.

ignorance, lack of knowledge >

retracting, taking back >

It is my custom to refer all my difficulties to you, Sir, for no one is better able to resolve my doubts and inform my **ignorance.**

I have never been present at an examination of Christians. Consequently, I do not know the nature or the extent of the punishments usually given to them, nor the grounds for starting an investigation and how far it should be pressed. Nor am I at all sure whether any distinction should be made between them on the grounds of age, or if young people and adults should be treated alike; whether a pardon ought to be granted to anyone **retracting** his beliefs, or if he has once professed Christianity, he shall gain nothing by renouncing it; and whether it is the mere name of Christian which is punishable, even if innocent of crime, or rather the crimes associated with the name.

For the moment this is the line I have taken with all persons brought before me on the charge of being Christians. I have asked them in person if they are Christians, and if they admit it, I repeat the question a second and third time, with a warning of the punishment awaiting them. If they persist, I order them to be led away for execution; for, whatever the nature of their admission, I am convinced that their stubbornness and unshakeable **obstinacy** ought not to go unpunished. There have been others similarly **fanatical** who are Roman citizens. I have entered them on the list of persons to be sent to Rome for trial.

<**obstinacy,** stubborness

<**fanatical,** passionate

Now that I have begun to deal with this problem, as so often happens, the charges are becoming more widespread and increasing in variety. An anonymous pamphlet has been circulated which contains the names of a number of accused persons. Among these I considered that I should dismiss any who denied that they were or ever had been Christians when they had repeated after me a prayer to the gods and had made offerings of wine and incense to your statue (which I had ordered to be brought into court for this purpose along with the images of the gods), and furthermore had cursed the name of Christ: none of which things, I understand, any genuine Christian can be **induced** to do.

<**induced,** persuaded

Others, whose names were given to me by an informer, first admitted the charge and then denied it; they said that they had ceased to be Christians two or more years previously, and some of them even twenty years ago. They all **did reverence** to your statue and the images of the gods in the same way as the others, and cursed the name of Christ. They also declared that the sum total of their guilt or error amounted to no more than this: they had met regularly before dawn on a fixed day to chant verses alternately among themselves in honor of Christ as if to a god, and also to **bind** themselves by oath, not for any criminal purpose, but avoid theft, robbery and adultery, to commit no breach of trust and not **to deny a deposit** when called upon to restore it. After this ceremony it had been their custom to disperse and reassemble later to take food of an ordinary, harmless kind; but they had in fact given up this practice since my **edict,** issued on your instructions, which banned all political societies. This made me decide it was all the more necessary to extract the truth by torture from two slave-women, whom they call **deaconesses.** I found nothing but a perverted sort of cult carried to extravagant lengths.

<**did reverence,** paid worship

<**bind,** hold together

<**to deny a deposit,** to pretend you don't have something given to you for safekeeping.

<**edict,** official proclamation

<**Deaconesses,** women chosen to help in the Christian church

Pliny rather naively indicates that he thinks that Christianity is disappearing and the pagan cults, the groups worshipping the old Roman gods, are becoming more popular.

I have therefore postponed any further examination and hastened to consult you. The question seems to me to be worthy of your consideration, especially in view of the number of persons endangered; for a great many individuals of every age and class, both men and women, are being brought to trial, and this is likely to continue. It is not only the towns, but villages and rural districts too which are infected through contact with this wretched cult. I think though that it is still possible for it to be checked and directed to better ends, for there is no doubt that people have begun to throng the temples which had been almost entirely deserted for a long time; the sacred rites which had been allowed to **lapse** are being performed again, and flesh of sacrificial victims is on sale everywhere, though up till recently scarcely anyone could be found to buy it. It is easy to conclude from this that a great many people could be reformed if they were given an opportunity to repent.

lapse, become neglected

Trajan's response was moderate for his time, and his disgust for anonymous accusations is very sensible. When he says, "They create the worst sort of model and are quite out of keeping with the spirit of our age," it shows that he believes that an emperor should govern with fairness and mercy.

You have followed the right course of procedure, my dear Pliny, in your examination of the cases of persons charged with being Christians, for it is impossible to lay down a general rule to a fixed formula. These people must not be hunted out; if they are brought before you and the charge against them is proved, they must be punished, but in the case of anyone who denies that he is a Christian, and makes it clear that he is not by offering prayers to our gods, he is to be pardoned as a result of his repentance however suspect his past conduct may be. But pamphlets circulated anonymously must play no part in any accusation. They create the worst sort of precedent and are quite out of keeping with the spirit of our age.

 Christianity was legalized in Rome by the emperor Constantine in 313 CE. For his biography, see Nancy Walworth's *Constantine* (Chelsea House, 1989).

66. School Is Hard Work

COLLECTION OF LATIN GLOSSARIES, 300 CE

This passage is from an ancient Roman textbook that was used to teach languages. The same passage was written in Greek on one side and in Latin on the other. The same kinds of books that were used during the Roman period were also used for many centuries afterwards. Although there was some squabbling in the ancient classroom, you can see that the students worked hard during a long day and took their work seriously.

See chapter 15 of *The Ancient Roman World*

I awoke before dawn; I arose from my bed; I sat down and put on my socks and shoes. I requested water for my face; I washed my hands first and then my face; I wiped them dry. I took off my pajamas and put on my **tunic;** I did up the belt. I greased my hair down and combed it. I put a scarf around my shoulders; on top of that I put a white cloak, and over that a rain mantle. I left my bedroom with my **pedagogue** and **nurse** and went to greet my father and mother; I greeted them both and kissed them. Then I left home.

< **tunic,** loose, sleeveless garment

< **pedagogue,** a slave who protects a child on the way to school (later it came to mean *teacher*); **nurse,** nanny

I went to school. I entered and said, "Hello, teacher," and he kissed me and greeted me in return. My slave who carries my books handed me my waxed tablets, my writing box, and my writing instruments. Sitting in my place, I smoothed over the tablets. I printed the assigned sentence. When I had finished it, I showed it to the teacher. He corrected it, wrote over my errors, and bid me to read it aloud. Having been bidden, I recited it to another student. Immediately afterward a fellow student **dictated** to me. "And you," he said, "dictate to me." I said, "First recite." And he said to me, "Didn't you see? I recited before you did." And I said, "You're lying;

When a student < **dictates,** it means that he reads aloud while another student writes it down.

you didn't recite." "I'm not lying!" "Well, if you're telling the truth, I will dictate."

In the midst of this quarrel, the little boys, who were so bidden by the teacher, lined up in two groups for their elementary exercises; one of the older boys gave one group of them syllables to spell. The other group recited word lists, in order, to the assistant teacher; they print the words and then print lines of verse. I, who am in the advanced class, was given a dictation exercise. When we sat down, I went through my word lists and notes on grammar and style. Called up to the head teacher to read aloud, I listened to his comments on narration, speech construction, and characterization. I was questioned about grammatical theory, and I gave my answers. "Do you say 'to whom'?" "What are the parts of a speech?" I **declined nouns** and **parsed sentences.** When we had finished this, the teacher dismissed us for lunch. After being dismissed, I came home. I changed clothes and ate some white bread, olives, cheese, dried figs, and nuts. I drank cold water. After lunch I returned to school.

When a student declines nouns, he learns the forms of nouns, like *man, men.* To **parse sentences** means to explain the function of words in a sentence.

Charles Freeman, J. F. Drinkwater, and Andrew Drummond's *The World of the Romans* (Oxford University Press, 1993) offers a lavishly illustrated survey of life in ancient Rome. The section "Growing Up" includes images of children's toys. The authors also discuss almost every aspect of Roman public and private life.

THE ANCIENT AMERICAN WORLD

Very few written records survive from the native people who lived in the Americas before the arrival of European conquerors in the 16th century CE. The notable exceptions are carved texts (inscriptions) of the Maya of Mesoamerica, that is, southern Mexico and Central America. Scholars find it difficult to understand the symbols in these inscriptions, but the texts seem to focus on astronomy, tracking the planets' movement for religious reasons. Once the Maya, Aztecs, and Incas began to use the Roman alphabet (the alphabet we use to write in English) to write their native languages, they recorded poetry, myths, and history in Nahuatl (the Aztecs' language), Quechua (the Incas' language), and Mayan. But this material was recorded *after* the conquest, when European ideas and Christianity influenced what the native people wrote. Some natives, or half-natives, also wrote in Spanish the stories they heard from their ancestors, and sympathetic Spanish priests who arrived with the conquerors tried to keep alive the stories of a world that was fast disappearing.

The book *The Ancient American World* examines inscriptions, sculptures, and monuments to reveal the ideas of natives before the conquest.

67. A Mayan View of Creation

POPOL VUH, WRITTEN ABOUT 1550

See chapter 5 of *The Ancient American World*

The Mayan people have lived in Mesoamerica for thousands of years, and their ancient languages are still spoken in Yucatan, Mexico, and Guatemala. They kept records of their history and religion in pictograph writing called hieroglyphs. (That term, which means "sacred pictures," is also used for Egyptian writing.) Though some Mayan hieroglyphs carved on temples survive, Mayan books were almost all burned by the Spanish Christian conquerors of Mexico in the 16th century.

After the conquest, some Mayans used the Roman alphabet to recopy some of their ancient books. The Popol Vuh is a sacred book written in Quiché, a language spoken by Guatemalan Mayans in an area also called Quiché. It was written secretly soon after the conquest, and later translated into Spanish. It was first published in 1857, 300 years after it was first written down. It contains Mayan views on the creation of the world and the gods' creation of human beings. Two gods, Heart of Sky and Plumed Serpent, create the world simply by saying the word "Earth."

inscribe, write; **implant**, insert >
citadel, fortress >

This is the beginning of the Ancient Word, here in this place called Quiché. Here we shall **inscribe,** we shall **implant** the Ancient Word, the potential and source for everything done in the **citadel** of Quiché, in the nation of the Quiché people. . . .

This is the account, here it is:

Now it still ripples, now it still murmurs, ripples, it still sighs, still hums, and it is empty under the sky.

eloquence, persuasive speech >

Here follow the first words, the first **eloquence:** There is not yet one person, one animal, bird, fish, crab, tree, rock, hollow, canyon, meadow, forest. Only the sky alone is there; the face of the earth is not clear. Only the sea alone is pooled under all the sky; there is nothing whatever gathered together. It is at rest; not a single thing stirs. It is held back, kept at rest under the sky.

Whatever there is that might be is simply not there: only the pooled water, only the calm sea, only it alone is pooled.

Whatever might be is simply not there: only murmurs, ripples, in the dark, in the night. Only the Maker, Modeler alone, **Sovereign Plumed Serpent,** the **Bearers, Begetters** are in the water, a glittering light. They are there, they are enclosed in **quetzal** feathers, in blue-green.

< **Sovereign,** supreme ruler; **Plumed Serpent,** the god called Quetzalcoatl; **Bearers, Begetters,** mothers and fathers; **quetzal,** a bright green bird whose feathers were used for the king's headdress

Thus the name, "Plumed Serpent." They are great knowers, great thinkers in their very being.

And of course there is the sky, and there is also the Heart of Sky. This is the name of the god, as it is spoken.

And then came his word, he came here to the Sovereign Plumed Serpent, here in the blackness, in the early dawn. He spoke with the Sovereign Plumed Serpent, and they talked, then they thought, then they worried. They agreed with each other, they joined their words, their thoughts. Then it was clear, then they reached accord in the light, and then humanity was clear....

And then the earth arose because of them, it was simply their word that brought it forth. For the forming of the earth they said "Earth." It arose suddenly, just like a cloud, like a mist, now forming, unfolding. Then the mountains were separated from the water, all at once the great mountains came forth. By their genius alone, by their **cutting edge** alone they carried out the **conception** of the mountain-plain, whose face grew instant groves of cypress and pine.

< **cutting edge,** knife; **conception,** beginning

Robert J. Sharer's *Daily Life in Maya Civilization* (Greenwood, 1996) describes Maya civilization from its earliest beginning to the Spanish conquest.

68. A Corny Story

POPOL VUH, WRITTEN ABOUT 1550

The Mayan sacred book, Popol Vuh, tells the mythical story of how humans came into being. After the gods created the world and the animals, they were dissatisfied and wished to be worshipped by more intelligent creatures. They tried to create human beings, first out of animals, then out of wood, and finally out of mud, but nothing worked. Finally, they used corn (for flesh) mixed with water (blood) to create people who could walk, speak, and work.

See chapter 5 of *The Ancient American World*

conception, start >

And here is the beginning of the **conception** of humans, and of the search for the ingredients of the human body. So they spoke, the Bearer, Begetter, the Makers, Modelers named Sovereign Plumed Serpent:

begotten, produced >

"The dawn has approached, preparations have been made, and morning has come for the provider, nurturer, born in the light, **begotten** in the light. Morning has come for humankind, for the people of the face of the earth," they said. It all came together as they went on thinking in the darkness, in the night, as they searched and they sifted, they thought and they wondered.

And here their thoughts came out in clear light. They sought and discovered what was needed for human flesh... the yellow corn, white corn came from there.

And these are the names of the animals who brought the food: fox, coyote, parrot, crow. There were four animals who brought the news of the ears of yellow corn and white corn....

And these were the ingredients for the flesh of the human work, the human design, and the water was for the blood. It became human blood, and corn was also used by the Bearer, Begetter....

Xmucane is one of > the "divine grandparents" who created the first humans.

And then the yellow corn and white corn were ground, and **Xmucane** did the grinding nine times. Corn was used, along with the water she rinsed her hands with, for the creation of grease; it became human fat when it was worked by the Bearer, Begetter, Sovereign Plumed Serpent, as they are called....

These are the names of the first people who were made and modeled.

This is the first person: Jaguar Quitze.
And now the second: Jaguar Night.
And now the third: Mahucutah.
And the fourth: True Jaguar.

And these are the names of our first mother-fathers. They were simply made and modeled, it is said; they had no mother and no father. We have named the men by themselves. No woman gave birth to them, nor were they begotten by the builder, sculptor, Bearer, Begetter. By sacrifice alone, by genius alone they were made, they were modeled by the Maker, Modeler, Bearer, Begetter, Sovereign Plumed Serpent. And when they came to **fruition,** they came out human:

< **fruition,** bearing fruit

They talked and they made words.
They looked and they listened.
They walked, they worked.

Elizabeth Mann's *Tikal: The Center of the Mayan World* (Mikaya Press, 2002) illustrates the buildings and culture of the huge Maya city of Tikal with photographs of its ruins and reconstructions of how it once was a thousand years ago.

69. Friends and Flowers

TEMILOTZIN, "POEM OF TEMILOTZIN," ABOUT 1520

The Aztec poet and soldier Temilotzin fought alongside his friend Prince Cuauhtemoc against the Spanish conqueror Hernan Cortés. After Cuauhtemoc had succeeded his uncle Moctezuma as Aztec emperor, he defended the capital, Tenochtitlan, until 1521, before being captured and killed a few years later. According to witnesses, Temilotzin was present at the siege and saw the execution of his leader. He then dove off a Spanish ship and was never seen again—no one knows whether he committed suicide or escaped.

Like other poetry written in the Aztec language called Nahuatl, Temilotzin's poem uses images of flowers and feathers. All things in the world are temporary—even the most beautiful—but friendship lasts. In this poem, Temilotzin introduces himself and gives his view of friendship: "we have been loaned to one another."

See chapter 12 of *The Ancient American World*

I have come, o my friends,
With necklaces I entwine,
With plumage of the **tzinitzcan bird** I bind,
With feathers of the **macaw** I gird,
I paint with colors of gold,
With trembling quetzal feathers I enfold
The totality of my friends.
With songs I encircle the community.

< **tzinitzcan bird,** a brightly colored bird

< **macaw,** a type of parrot

< **the totality,** all

I will bring it into the palace,
There will we all be,
Until we have gone to the region of the dead.
Thus we have been loaned to one another.

Now I have come,
I am standing,
I will compose songs,
make the songs burst forth,
for you, my friends.
I am sent from God,
I have flowers,
I am Temilotzin,
I have come to make friends here.

Daily Life of the Aztecs: People of the Sun and Earth (Greenwood, 1998), by David Carrasco with Scott Sessions, examines the philosophy, religion, and everyday life of the ancient Aztecs.

70. Aztecs as Shopaholics

“

BERNAL DÍAZ, THE CONQUEST OF NEW SPAIN, 1576

See chapter 12 of *The Ancient American World*

Bernal Díaz first went to the New World as a soldier, accompanying Cortés during his conquest of Mexico. Díaz fought more than 100 battles and later settled on an estate in Guatemala, where he died in about 1580—more than 65 years after he first came to the Americas. Late in life, Díaz became angry at the official histories of the conquest, which gave all the credit to Cortés and his generals instead of to the soldiers. Díaz decided to write his own version—an exciting adventure in which ordinary soldiers play a vital part.

Díaz had an excellent visual memory, so his descriptions of what the Spanish found at the Aztec capital of Tenochtitlan are invaluable. Though he was a Spaniard, his many decades in the New World made Díaz more sympathetic than most Europeans to the native people and their culture. His description of the Aztec market shows that the Aztecs engaged in a large amount of trade even before the conquest.

Let us begin with the dealers in gold, silver, and precious stones, feathers, cloaks, and embroidered goods, and male and female slaves who are also sold there. They bring as many slaves to be sold in that market as the Portuguese bring black people from **Guinea.** Some are brought there attached to long poles by means of collars round their necks to prevent them from escaping, but others are left loose. Next there were those who sold coarser cloth, and cotton goods and fabrics made of twisted thread, and there were chocolate merchants with their chocolate.

< **Guinea** is an area in West Africa.

In this way you could see every kind of merchandise to be found anywhere in New Spain, laid out in the same way as goods are laid out in my own district of **Medina del Campo,** a center for fairs, where each line of stalls has its own particular sort. So it was in this great market. There were those who sold **sisal** cloth and ropes and the sandals they wear on their feet, which are made from the same plant. All these were kept in one part of the market, in the place assigned to them, and in another part were skins of tigers and lions, otters, jackals, and deer, badgers, mountain cats, and other wild animals, some **tanned** and some untanned, and other classes of merchandise.

< **Medina del Campo** is a city in Spain.

< **sisal,** a strong, white fiber

< **tanned,** made into leather

Frances Berdan's *The Aztecs* (Chelsea House, 1989) examines the culture, history, and changing fortunes of the Aztecs.

71. Scenic Views from an Aztec Pyramid

BERNAL DÍAZ, THE CONQUEST OF NEW SPAIN, 1576

Díaz accompanied Cortés as he climbed to meet the Aztec emperor Moctezuma at the top of the pyramid where he performed human sacrifice to honor the Aztec gods. Díaz therefore regarded the building as "accursed" for all the innocent blood spilled there. After the conquest, the Spanish destroyed the pyramid and built the plaza and cathedral of Mexico City on that spot, where they still remain.

See chapter 12 of *The Ancient American World*

When we arrived near the great temple and before we had climbed a single step, the great Moctezuma sent six priests and two chieftains down from the top, where he was making his sacrifices, to escort our Captain; and as he climbed the steps, of which there one hundred and fourteen, they tried to take him by the arms to help him up in the same way as they helped Moctezuma, thinking he might be tired, but he would not let them near him.

The top of the pyramid formed an open square on which stood something like a platform, and it was here that the great stones stood on which they placed the poor Indians for sacrifice. Here also was a massive image like a dragon, and other hideous figures, and a great deal of blood that had been spilled that day. Emerging in the company of two priests from the shrine which houses his accursed images, Moctezuma made a deep bow to us all and said: "My lord, you must be tired after climbing this great pyramid of ours." And Cortés replied that none of us were ever exhausted by anything. Then Moctezuma took him by the hand, and told him to look at his great city and all the other cities standing in the water, and the many others on the land round the lake; and he said that if Cortés had not had a good view of the great market-place he could see it better from where he now was.

So we stood there looking, because that huge accursed pyramid stood so high that it dominated everything. . . . We saw pyramids and shrines in these cities that looked like gleaming white towers and castles: a marvelous sight. All the houses had flat roofs, and on the **causeways** were other small towers and shrines built like fortresses.

causeways, roads crossing the lake

Having examined and considered all that we had seen, we turned back to the great market and the swarm of people buying and selling. The mere murmur of their voices talking was loud enough to be heard more than three miles away. Some of our soldiers who had been in many parts of the world, in **Constantinople,** in Rome, and all over Italy, said that they had never seen a market so well laid out, so large, so orderly, and so full of people.

Constantinople was the largest city in Europe and capital of the Byzantine Empire until 1453.

Cortés and the Conquest of the Aztec Empire in World History (Enslow, 2001), by Charles Flowers, provides a clear account of Aztec civilization and how Cortés was able to conquer Moctezuma so easily.

72. Play Ball!

FRAY BERNARDINO DE SAHAGÚN, FLORENTINE CODEX, 1577

See chapter 2 of *The Ancient American World*

In the years after the Spanish conquest of Central and South America, the priest and scholar Bernardino de Sahagún collected from a group of Aztec nobles—they called themselves Mexica, from which the name Mexico comes— their memories of their culture and the conquest. Sahagún organized this material as an encyclopedia with sections on history, religion, the calendar, and the people. The collection was written in the Aztec language, Nahuatl, and also contained hundreds of small drawings to accompany the descriptions.

Sahagún, who spoke Nahuatl, was among the priests who wished to keep native languages alive, yet we cannot know to what degree the Spanish priest shaped these native "memories" in his book. The manuscript is now called the Florentine Codex, because it is kept in a library in Florence, Italy. "Codex" is a word meaning an ancient manuscript in book form. In this section, Sahagún describes the ball game the Mexica nobles liked to play and the enormous bets they made on their contests.

Tenth Chapter, in which is told how the rulers took their pleasure.

They played ball. There were his ball-catchers and his ball-players. They **wagered** in this game all manner of costly goods—gold, golden necklaces, green stone, fine turquoise, slaves, precious capes, valuable **breech clouts,** cultivated fields, houses, leather leg bands, gold bracelets, arm bands of quetzal feathers, duck feather capes, **bales of cacao**—these were wagered there in the game called *tlachtli.*

< **wagered**, bet

< **breech clouts,** loincloths

< **Bales of cacao** are bunches of the seeds used to make chocolate.

On the two sides, on either hand, it was limited by walls, very well made, in that the walls and floor were smoothed. And there, in the very center of the ball court, was a line, drawn upon the ground. And on the walls were two stone, ball court rings. He who played caused the ball to enter there; he caused it to go in. Then he won all the costly goods, and he won everything from all who watched there in the ball court. His equipment was the rubber ball, the leather gloves, **girdles**, and leather hip guards.

< **girdle,** a garment that goes around the waist

The colored illustrations in the Florentine Codex give insight into how the Aztecs viewed themselves. The Medicea Laurenziana Library in Florence, where the manuscript is kept, has made several of these illustrations available on its website: www.finns-books.com/florent.htm.

73. Add a Touch of Toad and Mix

HUÁMAN POMA DE AYALA, LETTER TO A KING, 1615

See chapter 20 of *The Ancient American World*

When the Spaniards destroyed the Incan empire of Peru in 1532, there were no native records, because the Incas had no written language. But as the natives learned to read and write Spanish, they were able to write their native language, Quechua, in the Roman alphabet and to record the memories of their culture. The native Poma de Ayala became a bilingual translator for Spanish officials. He wrote a long account—more than a thousand pages—of the government in Peru and sent it to the king of Spain. He wished to criticize the cruelty of Spanish officials and make suggestions for improvement. In this passage, Poma de Ayala tells how the Incan king used magicians to poison his enemies, and that such men still existed in Peru under Spanish rule.

The account is written in Spanish, though Poma, who was proud of his royal Incan blood, uses many words from his native Quechua as well as his own drawings. Poma claimed that his father had saved a Spanish officer and took the name de Ayala *from him. His book survives in manuscript in the Royal Library of Copenhagen, Denmark, where it was rediscovered 300 years after it was written.*

quacks, people who pretend to be doctors

retained, used

One class of magicians which used to be found, and still is found, in Peru consists of evil characters who use poison for killing. These **quacks** sometimes do their work quickly and sometimes more slowly, so that the victim takes a whole year to dry up until he becomes as thin as a bean-pole and expires. Originally only the Inca **retained** the services of this sort of magician.

Another class of magicians was skilled in making men and women fall in love, or making men generous in their treatment of women. This spell was worked by burning grease and nameless dirt in a brand-new pot which was exposed to intense heat. A demon then materialized and carried out the required sorcery. Similarly, married couples or lovers could be estranged from one another with the help of the demons. . . .

Another form of witchcraft, still used today, consists in poisoning people with the venom of toads and snakes. Alternatively, a toad is caught, its mouth and eyes stitched with thorns and its feet tied together. It is then buried in a hole underneath where an enemy is in the habit of sitting, with the idea that he should suffer and die in the same manner as the buried toad. Some magicians keep toads and snakes in captivity so as to make use of them in this way. . . .

The most important of the magicians formed part of the Inca's **retinue** and these high priests were adored and respected for their supernatural powers.

< **retinue,** group of attendants

According to all accounts, it was their custom to take a new stewpot and first of all warm it while empty. Then they put into it fat, maize, coca and other foods, with some gold and silver. The contents were heated up until they were burnt and charred. At that stage the priests were able to talk to demons who remained inside the pot. They asked questions and received answers about how to make men and women fall in love and how to poison enemies. This was also the means by which they knew of future events. The male and female priests, once they had talked to these demons out of Hell, were able to divine everything which existed or was about to occur in the whole of the world.

The Royal Library of Copenhagen has a large website (www.kb.dk/elib/mss/poma/index.htm) devoted to Poma's book. There you can see almost 400 drawings by the author himself.

74. Manco Capac, the First Inca

GARCILASO DE LA VEGA, EL INCA, ROYAL COMMENTARIES OF THE INCAS, 1617

Garcilaso is one of the few native writers about the Incas. He was born shortly after the conquest to the niece of the Incan emperor; his father was a Spanish officer. He was one of the earliest mestizos—mixed-race Spanish and native—to become literate; he referred to

See chapter 13 of *The Ancient American World*

himself as "El Inca," the Inca. He went to Spain as a soldier and there wrote a history of Incan civilization before the arrival of the Spaniards. He was thus one of the first Americans to write about America.

As a descendent of Incan emperors, Garcilaso was proud to recount the birth, growth, and fall of the empire from its legendary founder, Manco Capac, to the execution of the last native ruler.

deity, god >

handmaidens, > female servants

conferred on, granted >

The first Inca king, Manco Capac, taught his people... [to] worship the Sun as their chief **deity,** persuading them to do so on account of His beauty and brightness. He said that the Pachacamac (which is the sustainer of the earth) had not placed the Sun above all the stars in heaven and given him these as his **handmaidens** for any other reason than that they should worship him and hold him as their god. He represented to them the many benefits the Sun **conferred on** them and how finally he had sent his own children to change their state from that of brutes to that of men, as they had seen by experience and would see even more clearly as time went by.

undeceive, prevent > from being cheated

On the other hand he taught them about the lowness and vileness of their many gods, asking what expectation could they have such vile objects would help them in their need and what blessings they received from those animals comparable with those they received from his father the Sun. Let them consider—for their eyes would **undeceive** them—that those herbs, plants, and trees, and other objects they had worshipped had been created by the Sun for the service of men and sustenance of animals. Let them notice the difference that existed between the splendor and beauty of the Sun and the filth and ugliness of the toad, lizard, frog, and other vermin they regarded as gods. Moreover he bade the Indians hunt out such vermin and bring them to him, and pointed out that such creatures should more properly inspire horror and disgust than esteem and adoration. With these arguments and others as simple the Inca Manco Capac persuaded his first subjects to worship the Sun and accept him as their god.

The Indians, convinced by the Inca's arguments and by the benefits they had received and undeceived by the evidence of their own eyes, accepted the Sun as their sole god, without the company of father or brother. They regarded their kings as children of the Sun, for they believed very simply that the man and woman who had done so much for them must be his children come down from heaven.

 Fiona MacDonald's *Inca Town* (Franklin Watts, 1999) uses the great city of Cuzco to examine the culture and daily life of the Incas.

75. Let's Decorate Our Palace

GARCILASO DE LA VEGA, EL INCA, ROYAL COMMENTARIES OF THE INCAS, 1617

Garcilaso's description of the Incan royal palaces comes from stories he heard from his mother and read in the works of Spanish writers, such as Pedro de Cieza, who saw the palaces before they were stripped of their gold by the conquering army. The lavish decorations included animals and plants in silver and gold.

See chapter 17 of *The Ancient American World*

The construction and adornment of the royal palaces of the Inca kings of Peru were no less in grandeur, majesty, and splendor than all the other magnificent things they had for their service. In certain points, as the reader will note, their palaces **surpassed** those of all the kings and emperors that have ever existed, according to our present information. In the first place, the buildings of their palaces, temples, gardens, and baths were extraordinarily even: they were of beautifully cut masonry, and each stone was so perfectly fitted to its neighbors that there was no space for mortar. It is true that mortar was used, and it was made of a red clay which they call in their language *llácac allpa*, "sticky clay," which was made into a paste. No trace of this mortar remained between the stones, and the Spaniards therefore state that they worked without mortar. . . .

< **surpassed**, was greater or better than

In many of the royal palaces and temples of the Sun they poured in molten lead and silver and gold for mortar. Pedro de Cieza confirms this . . . and I am glad to be able to **adduce** the evidence of Spanish historians in support of what I saw. These substances were used to add majesty to the buildings, which was the chief cause of their total destruction: as these metals were found in some of them, they were all pulled down by seekers for gold and silver, though the buildings themselves were so finely constructed of such solid stone

< **adduce**, give as a reason or proof

that they would have lasted for centuries if they had been left. . . . The temples of the Sun and the royal apartments, wherever they existed, were lined with plates of gold, and many gold and silver figures copied from life—of men and women, birds of the air and waterfowl, and wild animals such as tigers, bears, lions, foxes, hounds, mountain cats, deer, **guanacos and vicunas,** and domestic sheep—were placed round the walls in spaces and niches.

Guanacos and vicunas are South American mammals, the first like a camel without a hump and the other like a llama. >

Elizabeth Mann and Amy Crehore's *Macchu Picchu: The Story of the Amazing Inkas and Their City in the Clouds* (Mikaya, 2000) gives an account of the Inca capital.

76. A Spanish Priest Denounces the Treatment of the Indians

BARTOLOMÉ DE LAS CASAS, A BRIEF ACCOUNT OF THE DESTRUCTION OF THE INDIES, 1542

See the epilogue (chapter 22) of *The Ancient American World*

Bartolomé de las Casas first arrived in the New World in 1502 as a legal adviser to the Spanish governor. He earned a grant of land as a reward for his participation in the wars against the natives, but he rejected it and became the most active defender of the human rights of the native people at that time. In 1512, de las Casas became the first priest ordained in the Americas, and he repeatedly returned to Europe to argue for the rights of Indians before the king of Spain and even the pope. He had some victories; in 1537 the pope declared that the Indians were rational human beings with immortal souls whose lives should be protected, and, a few years later, the Spanish king Charles I banned slavery in the New World. But the ranchers needed labor, and slave traders later imported African slaves to work on the plantations.

De las Casas's book is a strong attack on the Spanish conquerors and one of the earliest documents on human rights anywhere in the world. His outrage came from his view that Spain's treatment of conquered peoples ran contrary to Christian teaching. For 50 years, he defended the Indians in sermons, debates, and books.

The Americas were discovered in 1492, and the first Christian settlements established by the Spanish the following year. It is accordingly forty-nine years now since Spaniards began arriving in numbers in this part of the world. . . .

God made all the peoples of this area, many and varied as they are, as open and as innocent as can be imagined. The simplest people in the world—unassuming, long-suffering, unassertive, and submissive—they are without malice or **guile,** and are utterly faithful and obedient both to their own native lords and to Spaniards in whose service they now find themselves. . . .

< **guile,** trickiness

At the time, they are among the least **robust** of human beings: their delicate **constitutions** make them unable to withstand hard work or suffering and render them liable to succumb to almost any illness, no matter how mild. . . . They are also among the poorest people on the face of the earth; they own next to nothing and have no urge to acquire **material possessions.** As a result they are neither ambitious nor greedy, and are totally uninterested in worldly power. . . .

< **robust,** strong

< **constitutions,** physical states, especially health

< **material possessions,** things

It was upon these gentle lambs, **imbued** by the Creator with all the qualities we have mentioned, that from the very first day they clapped eyes on them the Spanish fell like **ravening** wolves upon the fold, or like tigers and savage lions who have not eaten meat for days. The pattern established at the outset has remained unchanged to this day, and the Spaniards still do nothing save tear the natives to shreds, murder them and inflict upon them untold misery, suffering and distress, tormenting, **harrying** and persecuting them mercilessly. . . . When the Spanish first journeyed there, the **indigenous** population of the island of **Hispaniola** stood at some three million; today only two hundred survive.

< **imbued,** deeply influenced

< **ravening,** very hungry

< **harrying,** bothering

< **indigenous,** native

< Today, the island of **Hispaniola** contains Haiti and the Dominican Republic.

On the mainland, we know for sure that our fellow-countrymen have, through their cruelty and wickedness, depopulated and laid waste an area which once boasted more than ten kingdoms, each of them larger in area than the whole of the **Iberian Peninsula**. . . .

< The **Iberian Peninsula** contains both Spain and Portugal.

At a conservative estimate, the **despotic and diabolical** behaviour of the Christians has, over the last forty years, led to the unjust and totally unwarranted deaths of more than twelve million souls, women and children among them, and there are grounds for believing my own estimate of more than fifteen million to be nearer the mark.

< **despotic and diabolical,** brutal and devilish

Francis Berdan's *The Aztecs* (Chelsea House, 1989) examines the culture, history, and changing fortunes of the Aztecs.

TIMELINE

The centuries BCE *and* CE *are mirror images of each other. The years go backward before the Year 1* CE. *So someone born in 2000* BCE *who died in 1935* BCE *would have lived to be 65 years old. On both sides of the "mirror," the 200s can also be called the 3rd century, the 900s are called the 10th century, and so on—*BCE *as well as* CE.

about 5.5 million years ago
The earliest known two-legged human ancestors live in Ethiopia

about 3.6 million years ago
Early human ancestors (hominids) leave their footprints at Laetoli, Tanzania

about 3.18 million years ago
Lucy (*Australopithecus afarensis*) lives and dies at Hadar, Ethiopia

2.5 million years ago
Hominids produce the first stone tools; the earliest members of our genus *Homo* live in East Africa

about 1.75 million years ago
Hominids begin to move out of Africa for the first time, as seen at Dmanisi, in the Republic of Georgia

about 1.5 million years ago
Hominids use fire for the first time, as seen at Swartkrans, South Africa

about 500,000–400,000 years ago
Hominids hunt big game for the first time, as seen at Boxgrove, England

Homo erectus live in the Zhoukoudian Cave, China

about 120,000–70,000 years ago
Some of the earliest modern humans live at Klasies River Mouth, South Africa

50,000 years ago
Many Neandertals are buried at Shanidar Cave, Iraq

30,000 years ago
People paint and engrave some of the world's first art at Chauvet Cave, France

25,000 years ago
People build mammoth bone shelters, weave clothing, and make ceramic figures at Dolni Vestonice, Czech Republic

BCE

before 10,000
People first enter the Americas

9000
Members of the Clovis culture hunt big and small game and gather plant foods across North America

about 8000
The last ice age ends, many animals become extinct

People start farming wheat and barley at the village of Abu Hureyra, Syria, and elsewhere in the Near East

People domesticate plants in Mesoamerica

about 7000
People domesticate the humped bull, along with wheat and barley, in South Asia; the earliest known South Asian village is settled in Mehrgarh, Pakistan

about 5500
People start producing pottery and using copper in the Near East and South Asia

about 5000
People herd cattle, sheep, and goats in the Sahara Desert, Africa

Maize is domesticated in the Americas

The earliest Mesopotamian settlements are built at Eridu, in modern Iraq, and other sites

5000–3000
The Yangshao culture flourishes in the Yellow River valley in China

3500
People construct the first cities in Mesopotamia, including Uruk; the wheel, the cylinder seal, and a class society develop in Mesopotamia

3300
Ötzi the Iceman is killed in the Alps

3300–3000
People invent writing in Mesopotamia (cuneiform), Egypt (hieroglyphs), and the Indus Valley (Indus Valley script)

3100
King Narmer, also called Menes, unifies Egypt

3050
The Early Dynastic period (Dynasties 1–2) begins in Egypt

3000–2000
The people of the Longshan culture in China develop fine black pottery, walled cities, and a class society

2900
The first Sumerian kings rule city-states in Mesopotamia

2800
People of the Indus Valley build walled towns and houses of mud brick in South Asia

2700
The Old Kingdom period (Dynasties 3–6) begins in Egypt

2600–2500
Egyptians construct pyramids as tombs for their kings at Giza in Egypt

2600–1900
People of the Indus Valley civilization in South Asia build houses of baked brick and a complex drainage system, develop a standardized weight system, and trade by sea with Oman and Mesopotamia

2500
People in eastern North America cultivate sunflowers, gourds, and other plants

The Sahara Desert becomes very dry; farming spreads south of the Sahara

The first palaces are built in Crete in Greece; Indo-European speaking peoples start to move across Europe and Asia

2340–2284
Sargon of Akkad creates the world's first empire, in the Near East

2200
The First Intermediate period (Dynasties 7–10) begins in Egypt

2094–2047
King Shulgi in Mesopotamia creates the first laws

2050
The Middle Kingdom period (Dynasties 11–12) begins in Egypt

2000
The first villages are settled in Mesoamerica

Indo-European peoples arrive in Greece; the Greek Bronze Age begins

1800
Massive architecture is constructed at coastal sites in Peru

Minoans in Crete, Greece, develop the writing system Linear A, which remains undeciphered

1792–1750
King Hammurabi of Babylon creates an empire in Mesopotamia

1766
Shang dynasty begins in China

1750
The Second Intermediate period (Dynasties 13–17) begins in Egypt, and foreign invaders, the Hyksos, arrive

1700
The Late Harappan period begins in South Asia, where people began to produce glass

1595
The Hittites attack Babylon, ending Hammurabi's dynasty in Mesopotamia

1570
The New Kingdom period (Dynasties 18–20) begins in Egypt, as the Hyksos are forced out by kings from Thebes

1500
The reign of Pharaoh (Queen) Hatshepsut begins in Egypt

1500–1450
The Mycenaean Greeks conquer Crete

1500–800
The Vedic cultures flourish in India

1479
The Egyptians fight the Canaanites at the Battle of Megiddo in the Levant

1450
The Mycenaean Greeks develop Linear B, a writing system based on Minoan writing

1400–1300
The kings of Egypt and the Near East create a complex system of diplomacy

1350
The reign of Akhenaten and Nefertiti begins in Egypt, causing religious upheaval and the worship of one god, Aten

1335
The reign of Tutankhamen, the "boy king," begins in Egypt

1286
The Egyptians, led by Ramesses II, fight the Hittites at the Battle of Qadesh in the Levant

1200
The important coastal sites of Sechin Alto and Cerro Cechin are settled in Peru

1200
The Iron Age begins as iron technology develops in South Asia, Greece, and the Near East

The Israelites and Philistines settle in the Levant

According to tradition, the Greeks fight Troy in the Trojan War

Bronze Age civilizations collapse throughout Mediterranean

1186
Ramesses III of Egypt defeats the Sea Peoples

1075
The Third Intermediate period (Dynasties 21–26) begins in Egypt

1045–771
The Western Zhou dynasty replaces the Shang dynasty in China

1000
King David takes power in Israel

Olmec sculptors create colossal heads in Veracruz, Mexico

Italic peoples enter Italy

900–750
Greek Dark Ages; development of the Greek alphabet

883–859
Ashurnasirpal II reigns in Mesopotamia, expanding the Assyrian Empire

770–256
The Eastern Zhou dynasty replaces the Western Zhou in China

776
The first Olympic games are held, according to Greek tradition

753
Romulus founds Rome, according to Roman tradition

750–700
The polis develops in Greece; Homer composes the *Iliad* and the *Odyssey* in Greece

750
The Archaic Age begins in Greece

704–681
Sennacherib rules the Neo-Assyrian Empire

700–600
The Brahmi script is developed in South Asia

685–643
Duke Huan of Qi becomes hegemon (local ruler) in China

612
The Assyrian Empire ends

600
The Early Historic period begins in South Asia

600–509
Etruscan kings, the Tarquins, rule Rome

600–200
A pilgrimage center flourishes at Chavin de Huantar in Peru

587
The Babylonians conquer Judah, beginning the Jews' Babylonian Exile

563–483
Siddhartha Guatama lives and teaches in South Asia

551–479
Confucius lives and teaches in China

539
The Persians conquer Babylonia

529
The Persians invade the Indus Valley in South Asia

525
The Persians conquer Egypt, beginning the Egyptian Late Period (Dynasties 27–31)

509
The Roman Republic is founded

500
Monte Alban, capital of the Zapotecs, is founded, and the first writing develops in Mesoamerica

490–479
The Persian Empire goes to war against Greece

479
The Classical Age begins in Greece; democracy flourishes in Athens

433
The Marquis of Zeng dies in China

431–404
Athens and Sparta wage the Peloponnesian War in Greece

399
Socrates is tried and executed in Greece

387
Plato's Academy is founded in Athens, Greece

359
Philip II becomes king of Macedon, north of Greece

338
Philip II of Macedon defeats Greek forces at Chaeronea

336
Alexander becomes king of Macedon after Philip II's murder; Aristotle founds Lyceum in Athens, Greece

334–323
Alexander the Great campaigns in the Near East and Egypt

327–325
Alexander the Great invades the Indus Valley, South Asia

323
Alexander the Great dies in Babylon, aged 32

323–30
The kingdoms of Alexander's successors flourish in Europe, Asia, and Egypt, in a period known as the Hellenistic Age

321–297
Chandragupta Maurya, founder of the Mauryan dynasty, rules in South Asia

300–200
Kautilya writes a political treatise called the *Arthashastra* in India

274–232
Ashoka, the Mauryan emperor, unites most of northern and central South Asia

266
Rome completes the conquest of all Italy

264–146
Rome fights the Punic Wars against Carthage in North Africa and defeats the Carthaginian general Hannibal in 202

250
El Mirador flourishes as the first great Mayan city

221
The Qin dynasty conquers China

202
The Han dynasty is founded in China

196
Rome defeats Philip V of Macedon

190
Indo-Greek rulers control northwest South Asia

133–121
Tiberius and Gaius Gracchus serve as tribunes in Rome

60
The First Triumvirate—Pompey, Crassus, and Julius Caesar—control Rome

58–50
Julius Caesar, the Roman general, conquers Gaul (modern France)

48–44
Julius Caesar rules as dictator of Rome until his assassination in 44

31
Octavian defeats Marc Antony and Cleopatra at Actium for control of Rome

30
Cleopatra dies; the Hellenistic period ends; Rome begins to rule in Egypt

27 BCE–14 CE
Octavian takes name of Augustus and founds the Roman Empire

25
Restoration of the Later Han dynasty

4
Jesus of Nazareth is born

CE

1
Teotihuacan, the City of the Gods, is founded in Mesoamerica; Tiwanaku, the holy city fueled on raised field agriculture, is founded in Peru

1–100
Early Jewish communities are founded in South India

9–23
Xin dynasty of Wang Mang rules in China

14–68
The Julio-Claudian Emperors (Tiberius, Caligula, Claudius, and Nero) rule the Roman Empire

69–96
The Flavian Emperors (Vespasian, Titus, and Domitian) rule the Roman Empire

70
The Romans destroy Jerusalem in Israel

78–101
Kanishka, the Kushana king, rules much of South Asia, promotes Buddhism, and trades with Rome

79
Mount Vesuvius erupts and destroys Pompeii in Italy

96–180
The Good Emperors (Trajan, Hadrian, and Marcus Aurelius) rule the Roman Empire

100–300
Gandhara sculpture in South Asia shows a synthesis of Indian and Greek artistic traditions

100–600
Moche culture reaches its height in Peru; its craftsmen produce masterpieces of art

142
Zhang Ling founds Daoism in China

184
The Yellow Turbans, a rebel group, mount an uprising in China

193–235
The Severan Emperors rule Rome

200–300
The Laws of Manu codify the hereditary caste system in India

215
Cao Cao conquers the Celestial Master state in China

220
Cao Cao dies, and the Three Kingdoms period begins

250
Christians are persecuted across the Roman Empire

263
The kingdom Wei conquers the Shu-Han state in China

280
The Jin dynasty conquers the state of Wu in the southeast, unifying China

284–306
Diocletian forms the Tetrarchy (Rule of Four) to rule the Roman Empire

304
Liu Yuan establishes the Xiongnu kingdom of Han

313
Constantine legalizes Christianity in the Roman Empire

317
The Xiongnu capture the capital of China; Jin moves south to found Eastern Jin

320–335
Chandra Gupta I founds the Gupta dynasty in South Asia

330
Constantine founds Constantinople as the new capital city of the Roman Empire

376–415
Chandra Gupta rules Gupta dynasty

379–395
Theodosius rules the Roman Empire and outlaws paganism

395
The Byzantine period begins in Egypt

426
K'inich Yax K'uk'Mo' arrives at Copan, Honduras, to found the Maya dynasty

454, 495
White Huns invade Northern India

476
The western Roman Empire falls to the Goths

502–549
Emperor Wu of Liang promotes Buddhism in China

527–565
Justinian rules the Roman Empire and builds the Church of Holy Wisdom in Constantinople

540
The Gupta dynasty ends in India

595
The zero is first used in Gujarat, India

600
Teotihuacan, the great Central Mexican metropolis, is sacked and burned

600–1000
The Huari and Tiwanaku empires flourish in Peru

600–1000
Settlers arrive for the first time on Easter Island (Rapa Nui), Hawaii, and New Zealand

606–647
Harsha, king of Kanyakubja, rules in South Asia

625–645
Xuanzang, a Chinese pilgrim, visits India

712
Arabs occupy Sindh in South Asia

942
According to legend, Topiltzin Quetzalcoatl founds Tula in Mexico

1100
Tiwanaku, the great highland capital of the Lake Titicaca basin, falls, in Mesoamerica

1470
Inca armies defeat their last major rival, the mighty coastal kingdom of Chimor in Mesoamerica

1492
Columbus "discovers" the Americas, already inhabited for 11,000 years

1521
Hernan Cortés and his allies defeat the Triple Alliance in Mexico

1532
Francisco Pizarro and his allies defeat Tawantinsuyu (the Inca "Land of the Four Quarters")

FURTHER READING

ARCHAEOLOGY

Bingham, Hiram. *The Ancient Incas: Chronicles from National Geographic*. New York: Chelsea House, 1999.

Brown, Dale M., ed. *Ancient India: Land of Mystery*. New York: Time-Life, 1994.

Connolly, Peter, and Hazel Dodge. *The Ancient City: Life in Classical Athens and Rome*. New York: Oxford University Press, 2000.

Cotterell, Arthur. *The First Emperor of China: The Story behind the Terracotta Army of Mount Li*. New York: Penguin, 1988.

Fagan, Brian M. *Archaeologists*. New York: Oxford University Press, 2003.

Fagan, Brian M., ed. *The Oxford Companion to Archaeology*. New York: Oxford University Press, 1996.

Hawass, Zahi A. *Secrets from the Sand: My Search for Egypt's Past*. New York: Harry N. Abrams, 2003.

Hessler, Peter. "The New Story of China's Ancient Past." *National Geographic* (July 2003), 56–81.

Lloyd, Seton. *The Archaeology of Mesopotamia: From the Old Stone Age to the Persian Conquest*. London: Thames and Hudson, 1978.

Moloney, Norah. *The Young Oxford Book of Archaeology*. New York: Oxford University Press, 2000.

Orna-Ornstein, John. *Archaeology: Discovering the Past*. New York: Oxford University Press, 2002.

Silberman, N. A. "Digging in the Land of the Bible." *Archaeology* 51, no. 5 (September/October 1998).

ATLASES

Manley, Bill. *The Penguin Historical Atlas of Ancient Egypt*. New York: Penguin, 1997.

McEvedy, Colin. *The New Penguin Atlas of Ancient History*. New York: Penguin, 2005.

Morkot, Robert. *The Penguin Historical Atlas of Ancient Greece*. New York: Penguin, 1997.

Scrarre, Chris. *The Penguin Historical Atlas of Ancient Rome*. New York: Penguin, 1995.

Talbert, Richard J. A. *Atlas of Classical History*. New York: Routledge, 1988.

FAMILY

"Children of Ancient Mesopotamia." Special issue, *Appleseeds* (October 2004).

Ebrey, Patricia Buckley. *Women and the Family in Chinese History*. London: Routledge, 2002.

Johanson, Donald C., and Kevin O'Farrell. *Journey from the Dawn: Life with the World's First Family*. New York: Villard, 1990.

Kaplan, Leslie C. *Home Life in Ancient Egypt*. New York: Powerkids Press, 2004.

Macdonald, Fiona. *Women in Ancient Greece*. New York: Peter Bedrick, 1999.

MacDonald, Fiona. *Women in Ancient Rome*. New York: Peter Bedrick, 2000.

Perdue, Leo G., et al. *Families in Ancient Israel*. Louisville, Ky.: Westminster John Knox, 1997.

Robins, Gay. *Women in Ancient Egypt*. London: British Museum Press, 1993.

Wroble, Lisa A. *Kids in Ancient Egypt*. New York: Rosen, 2003.

GOVERNMENT AND POLITICS

Levi, Jean. *The Chinese Emperor.* Trans. Barbara Bray. New York: Vintage, 1989.

Morkot, Robert G. *The Black Pharaohs: Egypt's Nubian Rulers.* London: Rubicon Press, 2002.

Roberts, Russell. *Rulers of Ancient Egypt.* San Diego: Lucent, 1999.

Versteeg, Russ. *Law in the Ancient World.* Durham, N.C.: Carolina Academic Press, 2002.

MYTHOLOGY, RELIGION, STORIES

Birch, Cyril. *Tales from China.* New York: Oxford University Press, 2001.

Black, Jeremy, and Anthony Green. *Gods, Demons, and Symbols of Ancient Mesopotamia: An Illustrated Dictionary.* London: British Museum Press, 1992.

Gifford, Douglas. *Warriors, Gods and Spirits from Central and South American Mythology.* New York: Peter Bedrick, 1993.

Johnson, Sarah Iles. *Religions of the Ancient World: A Guide.* Cambridge, Mass.: Belknap Press, 2004.

Martell, Hazel Mary. *The Myths and Civilization of the Ancient Greeks.* New York: McGraw Hill, 1998.

McCaughrean, Geraldine. *Roman Myths.* New York: Margaret K. McElderry, 2001.

Wangu, Madhu Bazaz. *Buddhism.* New York: Facts on File, 2002.

Wangu, Madhu Bazaz. *Hinduism.* New York: Facts on File, 2001.

Wilkinson, Richard H. *The Complete Gods and Goddesses of Ancient Egypt.* London: Thames and Hudson, 2003.

SCIENCE AND PHILOSOPHY

Anderson, Margaret J., and Karen F. Stephenson. *Scientists of the Ancient World.* Berkeley Heights, N.J.: Enslow, 1999.

Beshore, George W. *Science in Ancient China.* New York: Franklin Watts, 1998.

Dawson, Raymond S. *Confucius.* New York: Oxford University Press, 1984.

Gedacht, Daniel C. *Technology of Ancient Rome.* New York: Rosen, 2004.

Moss, Carol. *Science in Ancient Mesopotamia.* New York: Franklin Watts, 1998.

Nunn, John F. *Ancient Egyptian Medicine.* Norman: University of Oklahoma Press, 2002.

Stewert, Melissa. *Science in Ancient India.* New York: Franklin Watts, 1999.

Temple, Robert. *The Genius of China.* New York: Simon and Schuster, 1986.

Teresi, Dick. *Lost Discoveries: The Ancient Roots of Modern Science—from the Babylonians to the Maya.* New York: Simon and Schuster, 2003.

Wiese, Jim. *Ancient Science: 40 Time-Traveling, World-Exploring, History-Making Activities for Kids.* New York: Wiley, 2003.

Woods, Geraldine, *Science in Ancient Egypt.* New York: Franklin Watts, 1998.

TRADE, INDUSTRY, AND AGRICULTURE

Gedacht, Daniel C. *Economy and Industry in Ancient Rome.* New York: Rosen, 2004.

Major, John S. *The Silk Route: 7,000 Miles of History.* New York: HarperTrophy, 1996.

Whitfield, Susan. *Life along the Silk Road.* Berkeley: University of California Press, 2001.

Woods, Michael, and Mary Woods. *Ancient Agriculture: From Foraging to Farming.* Minneapolis: Runestone, 2000.

WAR

Anglim, Simon, and Phyllis G. Jestice. *Fighting Techniques of the Ancient World (3000 B.C. to 500 A.D.): Equipment, Combat Skills, and Tactics.* New York: Thomas Dunne, 2003.

Connolly, Peter. *The Legionary.* New York: Oxford University Press, 1998.

Millard, Anne, and Mark Bergin. *Going to War in Ancient Egypt.* London: Franklin Watts, 2000.

Morrison, J. S., et al. *The Athenian Trireme: The Historical Reconstruction of an Ancient Greek Warship.* New York: Cambridge University Press, 2000.

Peers, Chris. *Ancient Chinese Armies, 1500–200 BC.* Northants, England: Osprey, 1990.

WORK AND PLAY

Auboyer, J. *Daily Life in Ancient India: From 200 BC to 700 AD.* London: Phoenix, 2002.

Brier, Bob, and Hoyt Hobbs. *Daily Life of the Ancient Egyptians.* Westport, Conn.: Greenwood, 1999.

Carrasco, Davíd, with Scott Sessions. *Daily Life of the Aztecs: People of the Sun and Earth.* Westport, Conn.: Greenwood, 1998.

Loewe, Michael. *Everyday Life in Early Imperial China during the Han Period, 202 BC–AD 220.* New York: Putnam, 1968.

MacDonald, Fiona. *Inca Town.* New York: Franklin Watts, 1999.

MacDonald, Fiona. *You Wouldn't Want to be a Slave in Ancient Greece: A Life You Would Rather Not Have.* London: Franklin Watts, 2001.

Nardo, Don. *Greek and Roman Sport.* San Diego: Lucent, 1999.

Nardo, Don. *Life in Ancient Rome.* San Diego: Lucent, 1997.

Nemet-Nejat, Karen R. *Daily Life in Ancient Mesopotamia.* Peabody, Mass.: Hendrickson Publishers, 2002.

Sharer, Robert J. *Daily Life in Maya Civilization.* Westport, Conn.: Greenwood Press, 1996.

WEBSITES

GENERAL ANCIENT HISTORY

National Geographic History and Culture
www.nationalgeographic.com/history/
Focuses mostly on ancient history, including important information about recent archaeological finds.

Seven Wonders of the Ancient World
http://ce.eng.usf.edu/pharos/wonders/
This site sponsored by the University of South Florida gives photos or artists' reconstructions and descriptions of the seven wonders of the ancient world, which were all located in the Mediterranean and Near East regions.

ARCHAEOLOGY

Archaeology Exhibits
www.mnsu.edu/emuseum/archaeology/
An EMuseum, sponsored by Minnesota State University, with virtual exhibits on general archaeology, artifacts, dating techniques, fieldwork, prehistoric technology, sites, underwater archaeology, virtual archaeology, rock art, and world museums.

BBC Archaeology
www.bbc.co.uk/history/archaeology/
This site provides a good overview of archaeology. Most of the examples are from excavations in Britain.

MUSEUMS

The Louvre Museum in Paris, the British Museum in London, and the Metropolitan Museum in New York all contain artwork and objects from almost every ancient civilization. Their websites feature illustrations of many of these objects.

British Museum, London, general webpage
www.thebritishmuseum.ac.uk/world/world.html

British Museum COMPASS
www.thebritishmuseum.ac.uk/compass/
A database of more than 5,000 objects from the museum's collection.

Louvre Museum, Paris
www.louvre.fr/louvrea.htm

Metropolitan Museum of Art, New York City
www.metmuseum.org/Works_of_Art/collection.asp?HomePageLink=permanentcollection_l

PRIMARY SOURCES

The Ancient History Sourcebook
www.fordham.edu/halsall/ancient/asbook.html
This website sponsored by Fordham University includes links to translations of innumerable sources from almost all ancient civilizations.

WOMEN AND FAMILIES

Women in the Ancient World
www.womenintheancientworld.com/index.htm
James C. Thompson, the sponsor of this site, discusses the lives of women in Mesopotamia, Israel, Egypt, Greece, and Rome.

EARLY HUMANS

Becoming Human
www.becominghuman.org/
An interactive journey through 4 million years of human evolution, with accompanying news and features and lesson plans.

Çatalhöyük: Excavations of a Neolithic Anatolian Höyük
catal.arch.cam.ac.uk/index.html
This site, sponsored by the Friends of Çatalhöyük—the neolithic settlement in modern-day Turkey—provides access to the diary entries written by the archaeologists who excavated the site.

Human Evolution: You Try It
www.pbs.org/wgbh/aso/tryit/evolution
Part of the PBS educational site "You Try It," "Human Evolution" lets you learn about the Laetoli footprints, the Leakey family, and more.

ANCIENT NEAR EAST

British Museum: Mesopotamia
www.mesopotamia.co.uk/
A wealth of information about the ancient Near East illustrated with objects from the collections of the British Museum, including palaces and warfare, astronomers, geography, writing, religion, royal tombs of Ur, trade and transport, and ziggurats.

Internet Ancient History Sourcebook: Mesopotamia and Israel
www.fordham.edu/halsall/ancient/asbook03.html
www.fordham.edu/halsall/ancient/asbook06.html
From the Fordham University site, primary sources from Mesopotamia and Israel including the complete Epic of Gilgamesh, Creation Epic, and Laws of Hammurabi, and extensive selections from the Hebrew Bible, among other documents.

Ancient Near East.net
www.ancientneareast.net/
Features links to websites for archaeological sites across the Near East as well as other resources and information.

EGYPT

The British Museum: Ancient Egypt
www.ancientegypt.co.uk/menu.html
Includes pages on daily life, geography, gods and goddesses, mummies, pharaohs, pyramids, temples, and writing with illustrations from the collections of the British Museum.

Internet Ancient History Sourcebook: Egypt
www.fordham.edu/halsall/ancient/asbook04.html
Primary documents, secondary sources, and images of art and architecture from ancient Egypt and Kush.

The Ancient Egypt Site
www.ancient-egypt.org/index.html
Created by the Belgian Egyptologist Jacques Kinnaer, this site allows visitors to explore more than 3,000 years of ancient Egyptian history, examine the sites and monuments, learn the language and the writing, and link to other sites.

SOUTH ASIA

Internet Indian History Sourcebook
www.fordham.edu/halsall/india/indiasbook.html
A collection of primary texts from ancient India, including the Vedas, the Bhagavad Gita, and Buddhist texts. It contains many links to other websites on South Asia.

Ancient Civilizations: India
www.ancientindia.co.uk/staff/main.html
A website developed by the British Museum for teachers and students. It has a great deal of explanatory material; for images go to the British Museum's COMPASS website.

CHINA

A Visual Sourcebook for Chinese Civilization
http://depts.washington.edu/chinaciv/
This site from a top scholar at the University of Washington has informative and well-illustrated pages on ancient tombs, Buddhism, calligraphy, and military technology, among other topics.

Internet East Asian History Sourcebook
www.fordham.edu/halsall/eastasia/eastasiasbook.html
This collection of primary sources is very strong in the area of philosophy, especially Confucianism and Daoism. It also includes links to many other primary sources.

British Museum: Ancient China
www.ancientchina.co.uk/menu.html
Topics covered in this website include crafts and artisans, geography, time, tombs and ancestors, and writing.

GREECE

Athenian Daily Life
http://depthome.brooklyn.cuny.edu/classics/dunkle/athnlife/index.htm
This site sponsored by the classics department at Brooklyn College provides information about different aspects of Athenian life.

Internet Ancient History Sourcebook: Greece
www.fordham.edu/halsall/ancient/asbook07.html
The site contains historical and literary texts concerning ancient Greece, including full texts of important historians such as Herodotus and Thucydides, as well as Homer and Greek drama. It contains links to many other websites on Greek civilization.

Hellenic Culture
www.culture.gr/
The official website of the Greek cultural ministry, with photographs of sites and objects throughout Greece.

ROME

Maecenas
http://wings.buffalo.edu/AandL/Maecenas/
Created by an associate professor emeritus of classics at the University of Buffalo, this site offers an extensive collection of photographs of Roman sites throughout Italy, France, and Britain.

Internet Ancient History Sourcebook: Rome
www.fordham.edu/halsall/ancient/asbook09.html
Historical and literary texts from ancient Rome, including full texts by important writers such as Livy, Virgil, and Plutarch.

Rome: Republic to Empire
www.vroma.org/~bmcmanus/romanpages.html
Created by a professor of classics at the College of New Rochelle, this site clearly explains many topics in Roman history, culture and civilization, and has links to images.

ANCIENT AMERICAS

Ancient Mesoamerican Civilizations
www.angelfire.com/ca/humanorigins/
Sponsored by the department of anthropology at the University of Minnesota, this site covers all the cultures of Mesoamerica, offering links to a wide range of other sites as well as fun games.

Dumbarton Oaks
www.doaks.org/PCWebSite/gallerytour.html
A gallery tour including about 100 objects in the pre-Columbian collection at Dumbarton Oaks.

Foundation for Latin American Anthropological Research
www.maya-archaeology.org
Information and images about the art, architecture, and hieroglyphics of the Maya, the Olmec, and the city of Teotihuacan.

A Precolumbian Portfolio
http://research.famsi.org/kerrportfolio.html
Sponsored by the Foundation for the Advancement of Mesoamerican Studies, this site has photographs of vases, bowls, and plates from various New World cultures, including South America, arranged by the site where they were found.

THEMATIC INDEX

SERIES INDEX

Page references are grouped by volume. The abbreviations used for each volume are AM (*The Ancient American World*), CH (*The Ancient Chinese World*), EG (*The Ancient Egyptian World*), EH (*The Early Human World*), GR (*The Ancient Greek World*), NE (*The Ancient Near Eastern World*), PS (*Primary Sources & Reference Volume*), ROM (*The Ancient Roman World*), and SA (*The Ancient South Asian World*). These abbreviations are also provided in the key at the bottom of the page spread.

References to illustrations and their captions are indicated by page numbers in **bold.**

TEXT AND PICTURE CREDITS

TEXT CREDITS

Page 24, 1955 translation of Hammurabi's law 148: Theophile J. Meek, trans., "The Code of Hammurabi" in James B. Pritchard, ed., *Ancient Near Eastern Texts Relating to the Old Testament* (Princeton, N.J.: Princeton University Press, 1955), 166–77.

Page 24, 1997 translation of Hammurabi's law 148: Martha Roth, trans., *Law Collections from Mesopotamia and Asia Minor,* 2nd ed. (Atlanta: Scholars Press, 1997).

1. Mary Leakey, *Disclosing the Past* (Garden City, N.Y.: Doubleday, 1984), 120–121.

2. Olorgesailie website,

www.mnh.si.edu/anthro/humanorigins/aop/olorg1999/dispatch/start.htm

3. A. M. T. Moore, "A Pre-Neolithic Farmers' Village on the Euphrates," *Scientific American* 241 (August 1979): 50–58.

4. Frank G. Matero, "The Lost City of Çatalhöyük" and "Preserving the Excavated Past," *Dig,* vol. 4, no. 2 (March/April 2002): 6–7, 8–9.

5. Konrad Spindler, "Ötzi the Ice Man" in Brian Fagan, ed., *Eyewitness to Discovery* (New York: Oxford University Press, 1996), 239–40. Originally published as *The Man in the Ice: The Discovery of a 5,000-Year-Old Body Reveals the Secrets of the Stone Age,* trans. Ewald Osers (New York: Harmony, 1994), 10–11.

6. Richard Daugherty and Ruth Kirk, "Ozette, Washington," in Brian Fagan, ed., *Eyewitness to Discovery* (New York: Oxford University Press, 1996), 310–11.

7. James B. Pritchard, trans., *Ancient Near Eastern Texts* (Princeton, N.J.: Princeton University Press, 1969), 579–82.

8. Samuel N. Kramer, *The Sumerians* (Chicago: University of Chicago Press, 1963), 237–39.

9. Andrew George, *The Epic of Gilgamesh* (New York: Penguin, 1999), 124.

10. Martha Roth, *Law Collections from Mesopotamia and Asia Minor,* 2nd ed. (Atlanta: Scholars Press, 1997), pp. 81, 82, 85, 91, 107, 109, 113, 132, 133, 134.

11. A. Leo Oppenheim, *Letters from Mesopotamia* (Chicago: University of Chicago Press, 1967), 84–85.

12. William L. Moran, *The Amarna Letters* (Baltimore: Johns Hopkins University Press, 1992), 50.

13. Genesis 2:5–3:23, Holy Bible, New Revised Standard Version.

14. 1 Samuel 18:6–16, Holy Bible, New Revised Standard Version.

15. Daniel David Luckenbill, *Ancient Records of Assyria and Babylonia,* vol. 2 (Chicago: University of Chicago Press, 1927), 185–86.

16. Bendt Alster, *Proverbs Of Ancient Sumer : The World's Earliest Proverb Collections* (Bethesda, Md.: CDL Press, 1997) and James B. Pritchard, *Ancient Near Eastern Texts,* 3rd ed. with supplement (Princeton, N.J.: Princeton University Press, 1969).

Proverbs, Hebrew Bible, 24:24–25, 28:27, 22:1, 29:3, 23:22, 20:4, 10:4, 12:16, 15:7, 16:18, 27:2, 29:11.

17. Richard B. Parkinson, trans., *The Tale of Sinuhe and Other Ancient Egyptian Poems, 1940–1640 BC* (Oxford: Clarendon Press, 1997), 251–59.

18. William Kelly Simpson, ed., *The Literature of Ancient Egypt: An Anthology of Stories, Instructions, Stelae, Autobiographies, and Poetry* (New Haven, Conn.: Yale University Press, 1973), 71–74.

19. Translation by Robert K. Ritner, in William Kelly Simpson, ed., *The Literature of Ancient Egypt: An Anthology of Stories, Instructions, Stelae, Autobiographies, and Poetry,* 3rd ed. (New Haven, Conn.: Yale University Press, 2003), 269–70.

20. James Henry Breasted, trans., *Ancient Records of Egypt,* part 2, (Chicago: University of Chicago Press, 1906,) 285–88.

21. John L. Foster, trans., *Ancient Egypt Literature: An Anthology* (Austin: University of Texas Press, 2001), 2–7.

22. Miriam Lichtheim, trans., *Ancient Egyptian Literature: A Book of Readings, volume II: The New Kingdom* (Berkeley: University of California Press, 1976), 69.

23. Edward F. Wente, trans., *Letters from Ancient Egypt* (Atlanta: Scholars Press, 1990), 134–35, 149–51, 160.

24. Lichtheim, trans., *Ancient Egyptian Literature,* 168–70.

25. Edward F. Wente, trans., *The Literature of Ancient Egypt: An Anthology of Stories, Instructions, Stelae, Autobiographies, and Poetry,* ed. William Kelly Simpson, 3rd ed. (New Haven, Conn.: Yale University Press, 2003), 117–18.

26. Breasted, trans., *Ancient Records of Egypt,* part 4, 861–83.

27. Robert E. Hume, *The Thirteen Principal Upanishads* (Oxford: Oxford University Press, 1934), 351–52.

28. *The Bhagavad Gita,* trans. Juan Mascaró (London: Penguin, 1962), 10–11.

29. *The Teachings of the Compassionate Buddha,* ed. E. A. Burtt (New York: Mentor Books, 1955), 30.

30. R. Chalmers, trans., *The Jataka or Stories for the Buddha's Former Births,* vol. 1 (Cambridge, England: Cambridge University Press, 1896). Reprint (London: Luzac & Company, 1957), #125, p. 275.

31. *A Record of Buddhistic Kingdoms; Being an Account by the Chinese Monk Fa-hien of His Travels in India and Ceylon (AD 399–414),* trans. James Legge (Oxford: Oxford University Press,1886). Reprint (New York: Paragon, 1965), 42–43.

32. *Kautilya's Arthashastra,* trans. R. Shamasastry, (Bangalore: Government Press, 1915), book 1, chapter 19.

33. Based on A. W. Ryder, *The Pancha-tantra,* book 3 (Chicago: University of Chicago Press, 1925), 324–26.

34. G. Bühler, *The Laws of Manu* (Oxford, England: Oxford University Press, 1886). Reprint (Dehli: Motilal Banarsidass, 1964), vol. 1, 87–91; vol. 2, 71, 73, 191, 194, 199; vol. 3, 55–57; vol. 9, 3–4, 24, 43, 65–66, 85, 328.

35. Arrian, *The Campaigns of Alexander,* book 5, trans. Ronald Mellor.

36. Kalidasa, *Shakuntala and Other Writings,* trans. Arthur Ryder (London: J. M. Dent, 1912), 63–65.

37. David N. Keightley, *The Ancestral Landscape: Time, Space, and Community in Late Shang China, Ca. 1200–1045 BC,* China Research Monographs no. 5 (Berkeley: University of California Press, 2000), 11, 14, 15, 23, 44.

Guo Moruo, ed., *Jiaguwen heji* (N.p.: Zhonghua shuju, 1978–82), text numbers 34229, 10124f (p. 14), 33337, 24225 (p. 13), 9627, 9500 (p. 11), 14138 (p. 44).

Zhongguo shehui kexueyuan Kaogu yanjiusuo, *Xiaotun nandi jiagu* (Shanghai: Zhonghua, 1980, 1983), text number 2666, p. 23.

38. *Book of Poetry (Shijing),* Mao # 154, trans. Jeffrey Riegel in Victor Mair, ed., *The Columbia Anthology of Traditional Chinese Literature* (New York: Columbia University Press, 1994), 158–59.

39. *Conversations of the States,* "The Conversations of Zhou," *Guoyu* (Shanghai: Guji chubanshe, 1978), 1/9–10. Translation by Terry Kleeman.

40. "Persuasions of the Warring States," *Zhanguoce* (Shanghai: Shanghai guji, 1978), 395–99. Translation by Terry Kleeman.

41. Confucius, *Analects,* cited according to the standard citation format for the Harvard-Yenching index edn.(Beiping: Yenching University, 1931–50). Reprint, (Beijing: Zhonghua, 1960, 1966; Taipei: CMC, 1965–69; Shanghai: Shanghai guji, 1983–88). Translation by Terry Kleeman.

42. *Strategies of the Warring States (Zhanguoce)* (Shanghai: Shanghai guji, 1978), ch. 14, "Chu," part 1, 14/482. Translation by Terry Kleeman.

Liu Xiang, *Shuo yuan (Garden of Explanations),* Sibu congkan chubian (Shangwu, 1919–22) edn., photorep of Ming Chuanputang [Transmitting Simplicity Hall] manuscript edn., 9/40a–b. Translation by Terry Kleeman.

43. Based on Ssu-ma Ch'ien, *The Grand Scribes Records, Volume 1, The Basic Annals of Pre-Han China,* ed. William H. Nienhauser Jr. (Bloomington: Indiana University Press, 1994), 155.

44. Wang Jia, *Shiyiji, (Record of Forgotten Events),* ed. Qi Zhiping (Beijing: Zhonghua, 1981), 6/154. Translation by Terry Kleeman.

45. Chen Shou, *Sanguozhi,* (Beijing: Zhonghua, 1963), ch. 1, p. 2. Translation by Terry Kleeman.

46. Liu Yiqing, *Shishuo xinyu jiaojian (New Account of Tales of the World),* ed. Yang Yong (Hong Kong, Dazhong shuju, 1969), 1/8. Translation by Terry Kleeman.